Selling Big to China

Negotiating Principles for the World's Largest Market

Selling Big to China

Negotiating Principles for the World's Largest Market

Morry Morgan

WILEY

John Wiley & Sons (Asia) Pte. Ltd.

Other Wiley Editorial Offices

John Wiley & Sons, 111 River Street, Hoboken, NJ 07030, USA
John Wiley & Sons, The Atrium, Southern Gate, Chichester, West Sussex, P019 8SQ, United Kingdom
John Wiley & Sons (Canada) Ltd., 5353 Dundas Street West, Suite 400, Toronto, Ontario, M9B 6HB, Canada
John Wiley & Sons Australia Ltd., 42 McDougall Street, Milton, Queensland 4064, Australia
Wiley-VCH, Boschstrasse 12, D-69469 Weinheim, Germany

Library of Congress Cataloging-in-Publication Data

ISBN 978-0-470-82597-6

Typeset in 10/14pt, Meridien-Roman by Thomson Digital

Printed in Singapore by Saik Wah Press Pte. Ltd.

10 9 8 7 6 5 4 3 2 1

This book is dedicated to my mother, who loves to argue; to Matt, who never cried when he lost an argument; and to Rio, who married me despite all of the arguments. Without you all I would never have learned the ropes.

Contents

Acknowledgments

It's not easy to write a book. It takes patience, focus, and a lot of bum-on-seat time. For someone like me, who subscribes to the Nike mantra—"Just do it"—sitting still for so long is a huge challenge. Those that know me well, particularly my parents, know that I like to work on many projects simultaneously, such as when I undertook my bachelor's degree at the same time as learning Chinese, joining the Australian Army Reserve, and opening my own company. Chaos is how I like to live.

But when my wife, Rio, got pregnant, I suddenly had a huge motivation to set a deadline. We'd both deliver "babies" of our own in 2009. So in July 2008 I started jotting suitable anecdotes into my smart phone, equipped with Microsoft Word, often as I flew between cities in China. By the time I had accumulated over 30,000 frequent-flyer points I had also written a similar number of words—all accomplished while in transit. The next step was to stitch it all together.

The hotchpotch of text was transferred into Google Docs. This allowed me to share access with friends and get rapid feedback. It also meant that I could access my work from my home PC, company laptop, or on friends' computers without having to transfer files, risking virus transmission, or creating multiple versions. Therefore, my first acknowledgment for the completion of this book goes to technology. Without technology, no words would have made their way to this page.

Now, of course, this book's gestation period was much longer than my wife's nine months. It was closer to two decades in the making. My next acknowledgment goes to Matthew, my schoolmate, who loved to argue as much as I did, and who taught me the value of evidence-based argument. Those were the days before the Internet, and opinions couldn't be supported with a quick visit to your favorite search engine. Encyclopedias, reference books, and back issues of *Time* magazine were used in our defense. That was great practice for my later life, as I realized microbiology wasn't my calling and moved into the debate-filled world of pharmaceutical sales.

This is where my boss, Michelle, introduced me to the concepts of needs and features, KOLs (key opinion leaders), and funneling. I realized then that having an ability in sales need not be innate, but could be learned, practiced, and mastered, much like playing golf.

My mother should also get a strong mention in relation to this book. She introduced many debating tactics, in particular the stonewalling technique. Back then, no argument of mine could penetrate her "but at the end of the day" statement, with which she could snapshut debates. When I was a teenager, she was my greatest opponent, and she taught me the power of building goodwill instead of blindly beating one's own drum.

And finally, I have to thank my business partner, Andy Clark, and my team at ClarkMorgan, both past and present. They continue to help me learn the intricacies of doing business in one of the world's fastest-growing economies and in a variety of changing cultures, and provide a sounding board for my sometimes radical ideas. They helped turn my theories into practice, and thus made this book possible.

To everyone, I'd like to thank you for your contribution.

Morry Morgan

Introduction

In 1978 Deng Xiaoping opened up China. The corporate giants rushed in—and many were even faster to leave. Difficulty in managing a Chinese sales force has been one of the main reasons for such failures, perhaps second only to poor marketing. This book is a step-by-step approach for managers of a Chinese workforce, regardless of whether they themselves are foreigners or local.

To be able to manage the Chinese, it is necessary to understand them, without overgeneralizing and without being about 20 years out of date. For many new managers who read about the Chinese, the workforce is both polite and diligent—a nameless mass of cogs turning the wheels of production—and to a degree this is true. Companies like Philips, Intel, and their suppliers house thousands of mainly female workers, most in their early 20s, in campus-like factory compounds comparable to those in the United States during the Second World War. The difference though is that this format of production hasn't changed much for the last 20 years in China.

But this book is not about the factory-based workforce. Rather, it is about the more complicated and generation-splintered Chinese that work downtown, often holding a university degree and dreaming of driving a Buick, or better still, a BMW. I say "splintered" because these generations are often completely different in belief systems, goals, and way of life, and regularly criticize one another in the media. Politically, China might be "One Country, Two Systems," but due to its rapid growth, socially, economically, and politically, China now has four very distinct generations. Understanding the differences is the first step to being able to manage a successful sales force in China.

THE CHINESE GENERATIONS

The working Chinese today fall into four distinct groups. Although each of these four generations was brought up under the same government, they couldn't be more different from one another.

Balinghou (八零后): The '80s Children

The *Balinghou* represent the generation born in the 1980s. By the time they became conscious of the world around them, suspicion of the West had been replaced for a hunger for all things foreign. To this generation, buying American, German, or even Japanese is not only culturally acceptable but a sign of wealth—and therefore success.

But while this generation is more open to change than their parents, many share the handicap inflicted upon those born post-1979. They are only children.

I've always argued that this shouldn't matter. After all, I am an only child, albeit somewhat older, and was brought up defending the position that having a sibling does not make one immune to greed and selfishness. I even lived with my parents and maternal grandparents, which is another coincidence I share with this Chinese generation. However, that is where the similarities stop. While I was commonly surrounded by families with two or three children, this generation has experienced singledom en masse. And the result is as could be expected.

With two sets of grandparents alongside parents who were born into scarcity, the *Balinghou* are understandably spoilt in a country that still had a GDP growth of 8 percent during the global financial crisis in 2009. This generation has grown up in relatively wealthy households at a time when globalization has meant that new foreign products were hitting the shelves monthly. It is therefore understandable that members of this generation are more open but less caring toward one another. What's more, they also tend to have a poor work ethic.

This workplace lethargy can be directly linked to the Chinese education system and its focus on obtaining the highest score in the *Gao Kao* (高考), or National Higher Education Entrance Examination, rather than preparing the workforce for work itself. The pressure to get into a prestigious university often means that morning reading sessions can begin as early as 7:30 a.m., with the final bell ringing as late as 5 p.m. In the home, an additional two to four hours of homework is very common, preventing the majority of students from gaining experience from part-time work or other extracurricular activities. Alas, while the examination takes nine hours to complete, twice as long as the American SAT, only three in five students will eventually make the cut and get into university.

Over 300 million students are enrolled in the Chinese education system at any one time (Ministry of Education 2003), resulting in classes two to three times the size of their Western counterparts, which further forces teachers to use rote learning as the overwhelming style of teaching. It's no surprise that the *Balinghou* are a tough group to manage, particularly in the field of sales, where self-motivation, lateral thinking, and teamwork are vital to reaching sales targets.

It's also important to acknowledge that while the *Balinghou* are the most modern of the four generations discussed here, they still have little sales experience. Their parents were often engineers or scientists, but most were more likely simply high school graduates, due to the 10 years of upheaval brought forth by the Cultural Revolution. While overseas Chinese are often typecast as born merchants, back in mainland China, this skill took a 30-year hiatus, from the time Mao Zedong shut the door in 1949 to the time Deng Xiaoping reopened it in 1978, and consequently the culture of sales and influencing skills is still relatively undeveloped. To highlight this knowledge gap, although Dale Carnegie's *How to Win Friends and Influence People* was published in New York in 1936 and sold 15 million copies, it wasn't until the early 1990s that it was readily available in its translated form in Chinese bookshops.

Children of the Revolution (1965–1978)

My wife was born in the 1970s, and I see a clear separation between her generation, which I've nicknamed "Children of the Revolution," and the younger *Balinghou*. For one, the Children of the Revolution, as their name suggests, were born in or just after the socially and economically disastrous Cultural Revolution, which ran from 1966 to

1976. Reflecting on this time, my wife can recount stories of receiving meat rations once a month, something that continued into the early '80s.

But while this generation had it tough at first, they were brought up by parents with positive Communist ideals, which include social harmony and cooperation. When Deng Xiaoping took over the country and announced an Open Door policy in 1978, it was also this generation that started traveling and interacting with the outside world. My wife chose to study for her postgraduate degree in Japan, and when she returned to China in 1999, she joined the ranks of the *Haigui* (海龟), or "returning turtles."

Technically, any Chinese who have lived or studied abroad could be classed as *Haigui*, however, it was the Children of the Revolution that were the original group who returned to the mainland with concepts of "best practice" and, just as important, an excellent command of English. This language advantage has allowed this generation to continue learning from the rest of the world.

In my mind, this is the golden generation, the people who have the advantage of holding the strong, socially conscious values of their parents and the ability to interact with the rest of the world comfortably.

The Old Red Guard (1950–1964)

As mentioned earlier, the Cultural Revolution was a social and economic disaster ending only after the death of Mao Zedong in 1976 and the launch of Deng Xiaoping's Open Door policy in 1978. The biggest victims of the movement were the students, who at the time must have thanked their lucky stars, but who ultimately lost 10 years of schooling in return for nationalism and unbridled freedom. Suddenly it was the worker who was "big brother" (工人老大哥; *gōng rén lǎo dà gē*) and demanded respect, and the schoolteacher was demoted to the lowest rung, as "stinky number nine" (臭老九; *chòu lǎo jiǔ*).

Today, these Old Red Guards manage many of the country's state-run organizations and private businesses, and often have their own distinctive style: a Polo branded shirt, slacks, and a man-bag—usually black and pinned under the elbow. A crew cut and a paunch complete the stereotype.

Managing this type of salesperson is challenging at best. They were brought up in a culture built heavily on relationships and not meritocracy, and in extreme cases feature in the press for taking bribes and embezzling government funds. And if you happen to be a non-Chinese, this group will also be quick to point out that you don't, and never will, understand China. Perhaps as a result of their restricted education, they never learned the Chinese expression, "You can't see the mountain when you are standing on it." (A view from afar is often better.) In a nutshell, this generation is both closed culturally and very selfish.

True Reds (1950 and earlier)

You are unlikely to employ this generation as they are of retirement age, but that doesn't prevent them from being your clients, particularly if you deal with, or sell to, state-owned enterprises (SOEs) or government departments. Both President Hu Jintao and Premier Wen Jiabao were born in 1942, putting them in their late 60s as I write this book.

The good news is that people of this generation are just as caring as their successors, the Children of the Revolution. However, they tend to be less open. True Reds have had most of the world posted as their enemy at one time or another, and now, without a direct foe, they can appear somewhat cautious.

SALES IN CHINA

Besides the four generations that you might be working with, it's useful to take a quick look at sales in general. Some of what I present in this book is common sense. Much is not. This is because the act of selling and negotiation naturally becomes a selfish process. Many salespeople equate "selling" with "talking," and that is wrong. The key to a successful sale (that is, a decision to buy), and subsequent negotiation on the nitty-gritty such as price, is to truly understand what drives the other party to make decisions—their *needs*. For that to happen, salespeople must first listen well enough to pick out the specific need from the mass of information that is being shared. And finally, they have to match that need to a *feature*. All this must happen before the parties can reach an agreement regarding the details of delivery schedule, volume, or price. That's right—an agreement only comes *after* the needs are met. It has very little to do with sales pitches and special handshakes. Focusing on needs is not a natural process, nor one taught in traditional sales books.

I should also add that while I wrote this book primarily with China in mind, almost all of the concepts are applicable to Western sales and negotiations. This is because China has been at the top of the list for the most attractive destinations in the developing world for foreign direct investment for most of this decade, and in 2007 it was ranked sixth of all nations. Accordingly, along with that investment came the expatriate senior management. I have therefore been able to test these principles on Chinese professionals and also on Americans, Australians, Canadians, Germans, Japanese, on British, Dutch, and French citizens, and on one Venezuelan. It's taken more than eight years of living in the People's Republic of China and more than 400 negotiations to be able to finish this book, and I hope to present ideas that will help you with your sales and negotiations—whether in Sydney or Shanghai, New York or Nanjing.

Before I dig into the details, I'd like to dispel two sales myths.

MYTH 1: THE B2B SALE

Regardless of whether you are selling Levi's jeans directly to a 16-year-old, or 9-foot-high tires to a mining conglomerate, at the end of the day an individual says yes or no. There's no such thing as B2B, or business-to-business selling. The whole idea that bricks and mortar, tables and chairs, and marketing plans can find needs, build goodwill, and negotiate for a win-win result is obviously ridiculous. However, somehow this acronym slipped into our sales vocabulary while we weren't looking. The fact of the matter is, businesses don't make decisions, individuals do. Regardless of what you sell or negotiate, you are always engaged in individual-to-individual sales, or I2I. I2I sales can also be thought of as "eye to eye." If you can't see eye to eye with a customer or supplier, there's little chance that you will both agree to a deal. Individuals have eyes. Businesses don't.

So, when I ask who your customer is, the answer is never "multinational trading companies" (even if you run a freight forwarding company) or "restaurants" (even if you have a customer service training company). Rather, the answer is always an individual, flesh and blood; somebody who comes to work in the morning and returns home at night. A real-life decision maker, not an address on a business card. It is these decision makers, the people I will from this point call *targets*, who actually decide whether to buy or not to buy. Nothing a salesperson can do, excluding injecting some kind of truth serum or holding a gun, will switch someone from "not buy" to "buy." The electrical signal within the brain of the target is independent of the outside world. The only person who can truly change that signal is the target. You know this to be true because you are also a customer. We are all responsible for the decisions we make.

MYTH 2: SALESPEOPLE CLOSE DEALS

Accordingly, the second fallacy that I'd like to dispel is the notion that a salesperson closes the deal. Interestingly, this misleading expression is not limited to the English-speaking sales field. In spoken Chinese, sales managers often ask their staff, "你搞定了吗? *(nǐ gǎo dìng le mā)*," which translates into "Did you settle the account?" Again, this implies that the signing of the contract is dependent on the salesperson, and not the target. Wrong!

Michael Hewitt-Gleeson, author of *Newsell* (1990), pioneered a different thought and even received his Ph.D. for proving that a salesperson *doesn't* close the deal. External examiner to Hewitt-Gleeson's thesis was Professor George Gallup, creator of the Gallup Poll. He wrote to Hewitt-Gleeson, "*Newsell* is the first new strategy for selling in fifty years. You have presented a new approach to a very old subject with proof that your ideas do work." Alas, twenty years on, Hewitt-Gleeson's theory is still relatively unknown by the majority of salespeople.

Of course, if you think abut it, you already know that it is the customer who closes the deal. As noted, we all know this because we are all customers ourselves. Even Jeffrey Gitomer, author of *The Sales Bible* (2003), agrees with the statement, "People don't like to be sold, but they love to buy." However, while we know that another person, say a salesperson, couldn't actually convince us to do anything we don't want to do, many unconsciously follow the conditioning that "salespeople close deals." Open deals, yes. But not close. It's true that for many of our purchases, the initial interest was created by the salesperson; the open. However, the decision to buy, the close, is an electrochemical reaction that takes place in the brain. Two lessons can be learned from this realization. First, as salespeople, let's not fool ourselves into thinking that we have Jedi powers that can change a customer's mind. Second, if salespeople can't control the close but have the ability to open, let's redirect our attention toward creating as many opening opportunities as possible.

In the following pages, I focus on I2I selling, discussing ways to build stronger relationships with customers, regardless of their nationality. This will ultimately increase your closes in China as well as elsewhere, because you will understand the importance of creating sales opportunities with real people, not businesses. However, to do that I need to first cover some new sales knowledge.

Part One

The Knowledge

CHAPTER 1

The Target Acquisition Equation

H ere are the ropes:

> Needs + Features = Benefits
> Goodwill + Reputation = Trust
> Benefits + Trust = Agreement × Price Quotient

The target acquisition equation (TAE) makes it easier to estimate the chance of a successful sale by breaking down each component into measurable values. I developed the TAE as a result of observing the sales process across the world, but mainly in Australia and China. These countries have strikingly different business cultures. In Australia, sales are relatively straightforward. Magazines like *Which Car?* have taken advantage of the public's increased understanding of their own needs in the search of a specific product, in this case, a suitable automobile. Australians are also a people used to asking questions, which may be why the country has a relatively high number of Nobel Prize winners, at 13, of which 11 were in the field of science. Chinese, on the other hand, are not the questioning type. This is even ingrained in the language. For example, the concepts of "question" and "problem" share the same word (问题; *wèn tí*). When I worked at Jiaotong University as a business administration teacher, my Chinese workmates told me they felt their lecture was inadequate if students, mostly *Balinghou*, asked questions at the end of the class. I felt the complete opposite. Initially at the end of each class, I would leave five minutes for Q&A, but this was only met with silence. Q&A soon disappeared from my lectures as well. Therefore the first part of the TAE, that is, finding the benefit, may be more challenging for Chinese readers, because it involves more questioning than is the cultural norm.

The second part of the TAE was developed in China, hence the "Selling . . . *to China*" title of this book. The text is still relevant to other sales and negotiations. The concepts of goodwill and reputation only became clearer to me when I found myself in China, a country that has the specific term *Guanxi* (关系), which equates to "it's not what you know but who you know." The fact that the Chinese have a term for this phenomenon highlights how important it is in their culture. (They also have an extraordinarily large number of words for tofu.)

Brands in China are also more immature, which means there is more white space for new brands to develop. Hence the importance of reputation, and the speed at which it can be gained or lost. Both eBay and Google sat on their laurels when entering the Chinese market, and they did poorly. While Google currently sits in second place behind Baidu.com, eBay eventually pulled out of the Chinese market altogether as it was unable to compete against its Chinese competitor, Taobao.com. Both American companies thought that their reputation could be transferred directly over to the Chinese market. Obviously, that wasn't the case.

So, once you show a benefit and develop trust you will reach an agreement. Well, almost. There is still one factor that could disrupt that—money, but more on that later. The elements of the TAE form the basis for the next few chapters.

CHAPTER **2**

Needs

Understanding human needs is half the job of meeting them.
— Adlai E. Stevenson Jr. (1900–1965)

I f you enter the name "Adlai Stevenson" in a search engine, you'll see that he was U.S. Ambassador to the United Nations in the early '60s. It's good to know that a man holding that much responsibility, particularly during the volatile Cold War period, understood that his primary role was to understand people's needs. This is also your primary role, as a salesperson or negotiator.

I don't want to discuss semantics at length, but to avoid confusion it's useful to point out that the term *needs* has a few synonyms in the field of sales and negotiations. Grande Lum, in *The Negotiation Fieldbook*, and Roger Fisher and William Ury in *Getting to Yes*, use the term *interests*. Jeffrey Gitomer, author of *The Sales Bible*, refers to needs as "buying motives." Please consider Lum's and Fisher and Ury's *interests*, Gitomer's *buying motives*, and my *needs* as one and the same. So what are needs?

Needs are (usually) hidden reasons for doing something. In sales, that "doing" is more specific; it means *buying*. However, don't confuse *wants* with needs. This is a simple and common mistake, so here's a simple way of explaining the difference.

Say you are in the market for a new mobile phone. The chances are that you already have one, so for this exercise assume that you lost

5

it. You want a mobile phone. This is because you want the ability to call your friends and send SMS messages. Of course, all mobile phones do this, so the salesperson in a Motorola shop can assume with 99.999 percent accuracy that you (or any Joe Blow or Wang Wei who walks in off the street) want a mobile phone. (Or are blind and want to buy a kilo of sausages, but let's not go there.)

But the target's needs are harder to determine. Here's a typical dialogue between one of my trainees and me to determine the need for buying a specific mobile phone:

"Why did you buy this phone?" I asked, holding up a Sony Ericsson.

"Because I like the functions," replied Sun.

"What functions do you like?"

"I like the MP3 player."

"And why do you like the MP3 player?"

"Because I like to listen to it when I am bored."

"Specifically when is that? When do you get bored and listen to the MP3 player?"

"When I travel to work on the bus."

"OK, but why a Sony Ericsson phone? There are many phones that have MP3 functions."

"Because I trust Sony Ericsson. I've used them before."

From this dialogue, can you assume Sun's need or, in fact, needs?

If you said "MP3 function" then you are incorrect. If you said "reputation" and "reducing boredom" then you are correct. The key with needs are that they are always subjective—that is, opinion. Sun prefers Sony Ericsson, because to him, Sony Ericsson phones have a great reputation. As you read this, you might object. That's fine, because, remember, needs are subjective. Just like the old saying, "Beauty is in the eye of the beholder."

Reducing boredom is his other need. Sun takes a lot of time to travel to and from work each day. There are a lot of ways to reduce boredom on public transport, and one is certainly an MP3 function. You could also match this need with "computer game," "video," or "word processor" functions. We refer to these functions as features. Features are fact, that is, objective descriptions of the object (or service, in some cases). They meet the needs, as in the equation, needs + features =

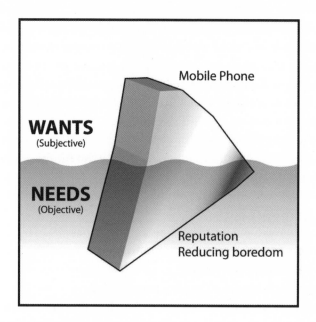

FIGURE 2.1   Wants and Needs Iceberg

benefits. But more of that later. Of course Sun might have more needs, but this is enough to go on with.

No doubt you know the role an iceberg plays in business metaphors. Eighty percent or more of an iceberg may be hidden from view. In my metaphor (see Figure 2.1), the top, smaller percentage, represents our wants. Sun wanted a mobile phone. Just like when you are hungry, you want to eat. Needs are hidden under the water. The submerged section of the iceberg represents needs. Sun needed "strong brand reputation" and "boredom reduction" and consequently bought a phone that he perceived as matching those needs. If you were hungry but short of time, then you might choose McDonald's or KFC. Alternatively, if you were hungry but had to finish a report, you might phone for delivery, or go to a café that has Internet access. Finding the needs of others is more difficult, because, as the iceberg metaphor suggests, people's needs are both hidden and the largest reason for decision making. You have to drop beneath the waterline.

My company provides soft skill training, but that doesn't mean that my clients need training. When they call me or one of my staff they actually only want training, like Sun wanted a mobile phone, or you want to feed your hunger pangs. Just as people can choose among many mobile phones and restaurants, my potential clients have literally hundreds of alternative training companies in mainland China and Hong Kong from which to choose. To be successful and win their business, I must be able to find the clients' need or needs, and just as the iceberg metaphor suggests, the number of possible needs is large, and they are often hidden from view. I discuss the how in Chapter 9, under funneling technique. For now I'll discuss the what. What are their possible needs?

POSSIBLE NEEDS

As mentioned earlier, I run a service business; one that trains the personnel of multinational companies in soft skills such as presentations, communications, and, of course, sales and negotiations. The first step to training new sales staff for my own company is getting them to complete a needs audit.

The needs audit is a list, the longer the better, of possible needs that a target might have. If you are conducting this audit for the first time, then I advise that you do it as a group brainstorm. There's a good chance that some of your sales team will not be exposed to all of the possible needs, so teamwork ensures that nothing is missed. I get my sales team to conduct a brainstorm on a regular basis, as new needs may develop that were not there a few years, months, or even weeks before. Take, for example, the needs that would develop suddenly if a target found out she was pregnant, or that her superior was stepping down. One minute the need wasn't there, the next it was. Remind your staff, as they conduct the audit, that needs are subjective and are different for each person.

The following sections present a needs audit for some of the more common needs that I've uncovered working in the training industry. I have also included an example of why that specific need was suspected.

Risk Aversion

Annie, like many Chinese, was *risk averse*. I had met her two years earlier when she was working in the human resources department of

Hong Kong real estate giant Shui On Properties, and when she moved to work for a large automotive company she gave me a call to arrange a meeting to discuss possible training cooperation. At the first meeting I was able to read (between the lines) that she was frightened. Annie was now responsible for the training and development of a much larger staff than in her previous role, and I could sense that she was stressed from the added responsibility. It was clear that Annie was not a risk taker. She needed to reduce as much risk as possible from her decision making. Her need was risk aversion.

Support (Process)

Jeff had been newly appointed to training manager of one of the world's largest financial services companies in its IT division, in Shanghai. This new role put him in charge of the training of more than 200 newly hired and young IT engineers. At the first meeting, Jeff informed us that he was the only member of the training department. This phenomenon is particularly common in China due to the country's high growth in GDP, and so junior staff are often given increased responsibility compared to their Western counterparts overseas. And this responsibility can include choosing suppliers. As a consequence, these new staff find themselves overloaded with work and so often look for training suppliers who can reduce their workload and assist with their daily routine. It was therefore an educated guess that support, specifically in relation to assisting in the physical process of the training, was Jeff's need.

Support (Knowledge)

I tell my sales team that they are not selling milk. They need to consider themselves as experts who add value by sharing knowledge gained from working in the training and development industry, not simply passing a carton across the counter and collecting money. It's amazing how many salespeople in the world give the impression that they are just order-takers. These salespeople take "the customer is always right" or, as they say in China, "the customer is God" to the nth degree. Consequently, customers begin to doubt the expertise of the salesperson, and sales begin to fall. So, if you're a sales manager, make sure that your sales force understands that they are an extension of your company's service or product. They are experts, or at least they should be.

Back to my business. My salespeople serve the HR departments of multinational companies operating in mainland China and Hong Kong. This department is relatively new, compared to the other functions of a company. It sprouted from the administration department as staff moved from being seen as a commodity to a strategic asset. The field of HR has even gone as far as declaring war—stating that there is a "War for Talent" between organizations, and that this war is damaging bottom lines. The HR evolution started about ten years ago in mainland China and continues to this day, and so—given its brief life as a department—many companies still have inexperienced people in decision-making roles.

Laurie was one such staff member catapulted to responsibility when a series of training managers cycled through the HR department of a multinational hotel chain in Shanghai—a gifted employee, but nonetheless inexperienced and now suddenly responsible for budget decisions. I was not surprised that Laurie's unspoken need was also support, but both with knowledge and procedures.

Convenience

Freescale Semiconductor finally signed a multi-course contract with my company. The HR manager made it clear from the outset that he was looking for a training vendor that could cover all subjects across all his company's locations as he didn't want the inconvenience of finding different suppliers in each city where his company operated. Convenience was a need that was held by this HR manager as firmly as by anyone dialing for home delivery or microwaving a TV dinner.

Scope of Service Area

After conducting a regional needs analysis on training requirements of senior managers, Microsoft went on the hunt for training companies that could provide communication skill training in Beijing, Shanghai,

Guangzhou, Shenzhen, Hong Kong, Taipei, and Seoul. Microsoft was somewhat shackled in that it had to use an official "preferred supplier" listed in its global supplier database, so finding a company that had the ability to train in four mainland cities, Hong Kong, Taiwan, and Korea severely limited the choice. Microsoft's need was clearly Scope of Service Area.

Control

"You can send me the information first," said Sally (not her real name) of Sanofi-Aventis. My colleague Leo and I had just explained that our company could create training reports that could be sent directly to the trainees. Leo could send this report after the training, but Sally said no. She wanted to have control over the distribution of the reports. It was clear that Sally's need was to maintain authority, or control, within her organization. Whether this was because she was afraid of losing her job or just something in her nature, it didn't matter to us. All we needed to do was match this need. This was easy, and it meant less work for us!

Experience

Scott was in a dilemma. Directors from around the world were coming to his Shanghai office to discuss the communication breakdown that was occurring between China and the teams in the United Kingdom and United States. The cost savings anticipated by outsourcing design work to China were being offset by indirect costs for redoing work caused by miscommunication between the three multinational teams. There was definitely a problem, he told me, but it wasn't caused by his team alone, and I concurred. I had seen his problem before, where home offices thought that the communication breakdown was 100 percent due to the other side, rather than room for improvement in the way their own team was communicating. Slang, jargon, and accents weren't the problem, these foreign offices thought. It was the English ability of the Chinese staff. The directors needed to know that all three locations had responsibility in improving communication, and it needed to come from a third-party expert on the matter, in this case me. Experience was clearly Scott's need.

Speed

Torres Wine was conducting its annual team building and product training at the Le Méridien Resort in She Shan, Shanghai. Sales had been steady that year, but there was lost opportunity and Lionel, the business development manager, wanted to turn loss into profit. He had convinced his boss to include a sales training on the last day and was sourcing a vendor. I met him on July 16 to discuss details that we had briefly explored on the phone. There was no hiding that his need was speed, since the training had been scheduled for three days away, on July 19.

Why am I confident that risk aversion, support, and the rest were the real needs of the customers in question? Well, there's no way I could know for sure, but each of the examples resulted in a contract being signed, and that's the greatest indicator that, like Adlai Stevenson, I understood "their human needs." Of course, this doesn't mean that a target may only have one need. More often than not, as with Sun and his mobile phone purchase, more than one underlying need is in play. Therefore, once you think you have uncovered a need, it's useful to continue to search for others. No one said sales was easy, and customers can be a fickle lot.

So far I've only talked about needs in relation to sales, but needs go two ways, so if you're a buyer, you should also understand the needs of your supplier. The buying department of a large IT company and I put together its own needs audit for suppliers providing peripheral computer components and servers. We came up with the following list:

■ Long-term relationship. Accurately predicting cash flow allows suppliers to reduce risk, while at the same time maximizing growth. Capital purchases, investment in more staff, research and development projects, or extensive marketing campaigns can only go ahead if the risk in increased expenses can be reduced by known income. A supplier contract guaranteeing a fixed volume of business through-out the year, or many years, is a possible need of many of this IT company's suppliers. Consequently, suppliers may be willing to offer a discount if this need can be met.

■ Shorter credit period. While I was writing this book, the global financial crisis had caused havoc, particularly to the Chinese province of Guangdong, nicknamed the "World's Factory" due to its role in pro-ducing much of the world's footwear, clothes, and IT products. Within a 12-month period starting in early 2008, more than 600,000 migrant workers had been laid off from factories in Guangdong province, and thousands of businesses had closed. This, more than ever, was a time that companies needed to reduce their credit to customers, to ensure stability or even survival. The IT company's procurement department could take advantage of this need and reduce costs by providing 15- or 30-day payment, instead of 60- or 90-day periods. This could be possi-ble because the IT company just happened to have a healthy bank account of US$6 billion.

■ Support (logistics). This IT company has a team of buyers whose job is to ensure that delivery of products is timely, and any lead time is managed via state-of-the-art software. This is a huge advantage to sup-pliers, who don't need to invest in their own systems, as this is a cost. If it's a need of a supplier, then it's an opportunity for a customer to receive a discount in return.

■ Support (R&D). Many smaller suppliers of this IT company do not have a budget for R&D. Instead, they rely on the expertise of their cus-tomers to help them develop new products and thus compete against their competitors. The team of buyers at the IT company informed me that this was often a need of their suppliers.

■ "Corporate green card." Securing the business of a multinational company can be the ticket to bigger markets. The first such client acts as an advocate, or key opinion leader, which reinforces the reputation of the supplier as reliable and therefore a suitable supplier for other businesses. I call this need a corporate green card, and this has been a need of my business in the past. Breaking into the lucrative Hong Kong market required my business to first secure a high-profile busi-ness. Korn/Ferry was our card, and it opened the door for contracts with TUV, EMC, and Bank of America. For any company, being a large multinational can impress future clients of suppliers. The corporate green card can lead to large discounts.

■ "Government red card." As you can guess by the play on colors, the government red card is the polar opposite of the corporate green card. (It has nothing to do with the term "red card" in soccer.) Foreign companies often wish to work with the Chinese government, which, while often more challenging than private industry, is no less lucrative. Arup, a British building services firm that has been involved in building city landmarks including the Sydney Opera House, London's Gerkin, and Beijing's Bird's Nest, Water Cube, and gravity-defying CCTV buildings, is one example of a foreign company that has had the need of winning a government red card in China. Both Siemens AG and ThyssenKrupp AG have received benefits from their investment into the Shanghai maglev train, under the joint venture corporation Transrapid. The Shanghai maglev was the first commercial project of its type, and is in no way a commercial success, costing US\$1.33 billion, but it has allowed both companies to open further government-controlled doors.

Back in March 2009, my company took on yet another "big hairy audacious goal" (to pick up a term from Collins and Porras 1994) in the form of Spark09 in Shanghai. Spark09 was a conference devoted to igniting new ideas, opportunities, and potential in 2009. The conference was aimed at kick-starting the year, which had been shrouded by the global financial crisis, and because people were penny-pinching there was no doubt that the event qualified as a truly audacious goal. To make the event even more audacious, we decided to run it in the tallest building in China, the Shanghai World Financial Center, to have 19 CEOs and thought leaders present, and to run the whole event with a budget of only US\$27,000 (CNY 180,000)!

So how did we pull it off? We focused on the needs of the stakeholders. The Web site design firm (In-House Web) and graphic design company (Studio Marque) had only recently opened and so their need was clear—to create a list of clients quickly and get their runs on the board. The PR firm, Adsmith China—like just about every other company across the world—had been hit by the global financial crisis, and so needed further exposure to generate business. And the venue, the Forum at the Shanghai World Financial Center, had opened its doors at the wrong time. Its managers obviously needed exposure and potential clients through the door.

We also targeted the needs of the speakers. When I was working in the pharmaceutical industry, I had seen how easy it was to attract doctors—both general practitioners and specialists—to speak for free at company-sponsored events. The need of these doctors was to be seen as experts, and the term *expert* can only be given to you by others. Standing in front of an audience of your industry peers, talking on your area of expertise, is a fast track to that title. I simply followed this rule with the 19 speakers for Spark09. Once the first speaker was confirmed, it took little effort to secure others who had the same need. What was most incredible is that the entire Spark09 event, from initiation to opening, took only two months to arrange. The same approach also allowed my company to conduct a Spark09 in both Hong Kong and Beijing—all this by focusing on needs.

Conducting a needs audit on your suppliers is equally as important as on your customers. This is because sales are taxed, but savings are not. A dollar, pound, euro, or yuan saved thus affects your bottom line more than a dollar earned. Therefore, you should have all departments, particularly procurement, complete a needs audit on both customers and suppliers.

NEEDS VERSUS POSITIONAL SALES

You may have noticed that I did not include low price as one of the needs in my list. I did this intentionally. People often think that this is the overwhelming need in business, and it's true that a need for low price is subjective and often comes up in sales meetings. But it is rarely the *most important* need. Let me reiterate "most important." It is certainly important, but not the number one reason why anyone makes a purchasing decision.

My theory that price is not the most important factor in purchasing decisions is supported by BMW's growth in China. In 2005, the *People's Daily* reported that BMW's China sales had grown by 52.4 percent on 2003 sales, compared to global sales growth of only 9.9 percent.

If price was the most important factor for consumers then this rapid growth would have been seen by Skoda and Lada, which also sell models in China, not a luxury car brand. Nevertheless, the misconception that price is the most important factor still exists in the Middle Kingdom. In case you are still a Doubting Thomas, here's a short (and true) story.

Back in 2006 I was training Swiss company Huber+Suhner's sales representatives in presentation skills. All 15 trainees were Chinese men in their 40s, and so I wasn't surprised when one of the trainees told me, "You don't understand China. Price is the most important factor in sales here."

As mentioned earlier, "you don't know China" is a statement commonly heard from the Old Red Guard generation.

"OK. Let me ask you some questions, then," I said, already knowing the answers, but wanting all the trainees to verbalize their irrational thinking. "Is your product the cheapest product on the market?"

"No," said the trainee proudly. "Our product is one of the most expensive."

"OK. So is your market share shrinking, staying the same, or growing?" I added.

"Growing," he replied. He was still smiling.

Silence.

The trainee's expression slowly changed as the oxymoron dawned on him. How could price be the most important factor for his clients when Huber+Suhner were one of the most expensive manufacturers in its industry and its market share was growing? Of course, that's impossible, but somehow many salespeople have been conditioned to think otherwise.

And the fact that low price is not the most important factor is evident as operating costs in China increase above those of Thailand, Vietnam, and much of the African continent, but foreign direct investment (as I mentioned earlier) still puts China at number six in the world. Investors consider reliable infrastructure, stability of government, adequate talent, and geographic convenience as more important than low price. There's also that enticing opportunity to sell to the huge Chinese domestic market.

Regardless, sales based on low price still happen every day, even with high-level negotiations. Several minutes into a sales call the salesperson is confronted with the question, "How much is it?" Many stupidly reply with the answer. The next thing the potential customer says is a statement rather than a question: "Oh, that's too expensive. You will need to lower your price." The customer has yet to know the benefits of the product or service, so this opinion is premature. Unfortunately for the poorly prepared salesperson, it may be too late to change the customer's mind.

These salespeople ultimately fail because they turn their sales call into a positional sale; a virtual tug-of-war with money. You stand on one side, holding the rope, while on the other side stands your customer. Every step forward is a loss to you, a price reduction. Every step forward for them is a price increase in your favor. In positional sales the salesperson starts the bidding with an inflated price. The customer cuts it down at the knees. Shocked expressions ensue until, lo and behold, the price is roughly halfway from the two opening bids. You've completely forgotten about the true value of the product or service you are negotiating for, and now the only consideration is price.

Positional sales are the overwhelming sales technique in China, and this is mainly due to the bargaining habit that exists to this day on the streets when buying everything from food to computers. Show a group of Chinese your new mobile phone, iPod, or laptop and the first thing they will say is, "How much did you pay?"—well before they ask you if you are happy with your purchase. At least one person in the group will comment that you paid too much, regardless of what price you say. It's no surprise that this habit flows over into business transactions. Positional sales also make a win-win result nearly impossible.

TARGETS

I've been using the term *customer* in my examples, but that is now going to stop. This is because the target acquisition equation applies to both buyers and sellers (which is why I didn't call it the "customer acquisition equation"). Whether you are trying to woo a customer or convince a supplier to give you a lower price, a target is a potential partner. They haven't signed the contract yet, but you hope they soon will. Either way, before you can find the needs you have to first find the target. This is not always easy, as often there are multiple decision makers.

Robert Miller and Stephen Heiman, founders of Miller Heiman, a 30-something-year-old sales consultancy from the United States, refer to these multiple decision makers as "Buying Influences." This is a synonym for target, but the team at Miller Heiman take their definition further by dividing influences into four types. I give a brief description here, and I recommend buying *The New Strategic Selling*, written by the two founders and an associate, for the complete description. In essence, here's what they say:

- *The Economic Buying Influence* is essentially the target who releases the money and has a particular interest in the bottom line. I'd go so far as to say that there could also be an economic *selling* influence who is equally interested in their bottom line, but with an interest in increasing the sales price.

- *The User Buying Influence* is the target who will ultimately use the product or service that you are about to hand over. I joke in my training courses that while it's well known that women, not men, are the major Economic Buying Influence regarding boys' and men's underwear, if it rides up, you know that Mom's going to hear a complaint from the User Buying Influence (the son or husband).

- *The Technical Buying Influence* is the target who's somewhat overzealous about checks and balances. These people are experts and like to emphasize their status by looking for faults.

- *The Coach* adds weight to your message from inside the target's organization. Unlike the other influences, the Coach is a benefit to your goal, not a hindrance. This role is essentially the same as that of my key internal influencer, a term discussed in detail in Chapter 6.

As I said, there's no better way to learn about these four factors in the purchasing process than buying the Miller Heiman book and getting the full and detailed definitions of each. However, in my experience, targets rarely fall into such fixed categories, and there is often some crossover. Therefore, I focus on the targets' hidden needs, rather than trying to force them into one of the four categories.

Finding needs is rarely as easy as asking for them. Most of the time needs must be uncovered by careful questioning called funneling, which I discuss in more detail in Chapter 9, or from a third source. You may be surprised by how much information regarding the needs of your target can be found from alternative sources of information.

ALTERNATIVE SOURCES OF INFORMATION

A wealth of information on your targets is trapped inside the heads of others—and you want it, because any major change in their needs will also change the complementary feature that you promote to reach a benefit. So, rather than rely totally on the targets to provide invaluable information from which to judge their needs, try tapping into the knowledge of receptionists, engineers and technicians, salespeople, and government officials.

Receptionists

Salespeople both in China and elsewhere often refer to receptionists as gatekeepers. Receptionists stand watch over the front door and telephone, controlling the access of all suppliers and customers. Very little escapes their watchful eyes or ears, which can cause headaches when you are cold calling. However, it does mean that when you are invited for a meeting, the receptionist can be a great alternative source of information.

Back in 2007 I was invited to meet with Alice Wang, the HR manager for Bayer CropScience, in Beijing. Here—close to verbatim—is my conversation with the receptionist on the day of the meeting.

"Hi," I said, "I'm here to meet your HR manager, Alice Wang. My name is Morry."

"OK, wait a moment," she replied and picked up the phone. "I will call her for you."

The receptionist spoke briefly into the phone as I glanced over the decorations on the wall, looking for company missions and visions or anything else that might help me during the meeting.

"She will be coming in five minutes. Please have a seat," announced the receptionist. My five-minute window for information had just opened.

"Great. By the way, you have very good English," I commended.

The receptionist blushed. "Thank you," she said.

"So where did you learn your English?" I continued, not wanting to give her a chance to find other tasks to do.

"At school."

"What about at work? Does your company give you training?"

"No, I'm not that lucky. Other departments get that."

Note: Can you see where I am going with this conversation?

"Oh, that's a shame. So what types of training do the other departments get? Perhaps I can talk to Ms. Wang and get you included." I smile again, this time half in jest.

"I think our sales team gets . . . "

I learned more about the training needs of all the departments from this five-minute conversation than in an hour spent with the target (the HR manager) herself. Of course, if the receptionist had answered yes to my question about whether she receives any training, I would simply have said, "Great! What type of training do you receive?" and then gotten her to elaborate from there. Either way, I would have uncovered valuable information.

On that day at Bayer CropScience, the receptionist outlined all the training that her company had received, and so by the time Alice Wang arrived, I had a list of departments who might be potential end users. In this case, the receptionist wasn't aware of the training firms her company had used before, but it was worth asking. Sometimes I've been lucky and a receptionist has even let slip the trainees' opinion of competitor courses, or the schedule for the next training. Armed with this information, I am much better prepared for my meeting with the target.

Receptionists are rarely trained in sales and negotiation—and therefore, if you are subtle about your questions, they are unlikely to realize that you are fishing for needs. Receptionists also have one of the more tedious jobs in any company, and the opportunity to gossip can make life more bearable on the otherwise boring front desk.

Engineers and Technicians

Other alternative sources of information are engineers and technicians. Like receptionists, they are often poorly trained in negotiation skills, and the nature of their job makes them focus more on facts and figures and less on the nuances of questions and body language.

In Shanghai a few years ago, I had an appointment with the foreign general manager of a supplier of mobile electronics and transportation systems, particularly for the automotive industry. On arrival, I introduced myself to the receptionist and attempted to get her talking about her company's training programs. My charms were ignored, and she flatly stated that she was too busy to talk. I should sit down and wait.

The GM's assistant appeared five minutes later and turned out to be a female engineer. Wearing a safety helmet and speaking near-perfect English, the Chinese engineer introduced herself and led me away from the foyer and through the maze of work stations comprising the various departments and then through the factory floor. As we walked, I asked her questions.

"So, how long have you been working here?" I asked

"Almost four years now. I like this job, although it's far from downtown," she replied.

"And what kind of training have you done in the past three years?"

She began to inform me that there had been a postponement of all training because a new GM had taken over. The new GM, she said, was ready to start training for the staff again and that was why I had been invited to meet him. I was the third vendor to visit that week. And that's when it happened. Slowing down her pace, she turned her head left so to look at me as we walked.

"My boss says that you are the best company for us," she announced. "He's interviewed quite a few companies already."

I can't remember saying anything after that. I was too shocked by how easily I had just uncovered this vital information. It wasn't necessarily the GM's need, but knowing that we were placed as favorites seriously changed how I was going to handle my negotiation with him. About 30 minutes later, after the GM and I had talked about the company's upcoming training content, schedule, and costs, he asked me if I could provide him with a discount. I told him that I wished I could, but that the price I had given him was the lowest. I let the silence that followed my statement weigh on him. Some may argue that this was a gamble, but I had done my research, and I saw no reason why the engineer would have lied to me. After a few seconds, the GM nodded his agreement to my price. He didn't know that I had also added a 15 percent markup between the reception desk and his office.

Salespeople

Salespeople can also be alternative sources of information, but, like you, they are often trained, or at least well read, in the field of sales and negotiations. Therefore, questioning a salesperson for information can be tricky. Thankfully, sales departments usually have a high turn-over of staff, so you may be able to find at least one naive newbie from whom to gain insight.

Government Officials

If you do business in China it is highly probable that you will have to have a meeting, or dinner, with a government official of some caliber. If you are fluent in Mandarin, then the task of acquiring information can be easier. If you rely on a translator, then it becomes borderline impossible.

A translator dilutes any goodwill that you are trying to build, and because of the delay in the translation, it gives everyone the opportunity to polish their response as they think more carefully before answering. My recommendation is to focus on these officials' lesser-ranked colleagues, who are often younger and consequently have a strong command of English.

But be warned. In some countries, particularly mainland China, there is a very fine and vague line between asking questions and espionage. As recently as July 2009, Chinese-born Australian citizen

Stern Hu was arrested on charges of bribery and stealing state secrets. The allegations relate to iron ore negotiations. There are also cases of Chinese reporters being arrested for as little as reporting the GDP ahead of official release. All I am saying is be careful.

Uncovering the needs of your target is the first step to displaying a benefit, and ultimately reaching an agreement.

CHAPTER **3**

Features

Facts are ventriloquist's dummies. Sitting on a wise man's knee they may be made to utter words of wisdom; elsewhere, they say nothing, or talk nonsense.

—Aldous Huxley (1894–1963)

Features are objective; factual. "We are the best soap powder company" is not an objective statement. It is your opinion. However, "We rated number 23 of all Fortune 500 companies, and no soap powder companies outrank us" is objective, and implies the same thing—that you are one of the greatest soap powder companies, if not the best.

Targets are more likely to believe objective statements, particularly those supported with documents, statistics, and photos. In essence, evidence. You'd think that providing evidence was obvious, yet incredibly, many salespeople go to meetings ill prepared, as if they can predict what kind of objections the target will bring up. These salespeople arm themselves with only their standard company brochure and a smile, thinking that these two items will be enough for a target to be convinced that they meet their need and therefore form a benefit. Unfortunately, more often than not, these salespeople are wrong; the contract goes to a competitor. What these salespeople need is a features folder.

THE FEATURES FOLDER

I first learned the value of a features folder while working for a Fortune 500 company, Sanofi-Aventis. Back then it still hadn't merged into its current name, and was known as Hoechst Marion Roussel (HMR), a German, American, and French giant. Michelle, my boss there, encouraged our team to do extra research on our products and collect evidence, or features, in the medical media. This evidence would be objective, as it was coming from third-party sources, and could therefore support the official messages displayed in our company's detail piece. As the name suggests, the detail piece was to be used to show the target, in this case a doctor, more details about the drug in question, particularly its effectiveness and low side effects. Armed with this features folder my sales team was then subjected to monthly tests ensuring that we could quickly match any need to multiple features and provide evidence for each feature.

When I moved from pharmaceutical sales to corporate training, I still maintained a features folder and continue to carry it everywhere I go. This folder takes up half of my laptop bag and is worth the weight. My sales team knows that it includes newspaper clippings, tip cards used for post-training, my company magazine, and even this book. It's heavy enough that it also doubles as my gym membership.

So as the sales manager, how do you create a features folder for your team? First, you need to do a features audit. You do this the same way you do the needs audit, as they will complement one another. Your goal is to have at least two features for each of the needs that you brainstormed earlier. Sit your team around a whiteboard and write down the facts of your business. For example, which year did your company first open? How many offices do you have around the world? Which awards did you win? Who are your top five clients? Second, think how you are going to prove each feature. When I say *prove*, I mean using as many third-party references as possible. Your own company brochure is weak in comparison to newspaper and magazine clippings. Photos of your senior managers receiving awards and actual samples that you have used with previous clients are great features, because they are objective. For your reference, I have created a complementary list of features to each of the eight needs that I outlined earlier for my business:

Need: Risk Aversion

Feature 1: We were awarded "Training Firm of the Year" in both 2007 and 2008, and this can be substantiated on third-party Web sites.

Feature 2: Our clients include BHP Billiton, ConocoPhillips, Ford, and Morgan Stanley, and a reference can be given for each company.

Need: Support (Process)

Feature 1: We can demonstrate our learning management system, Open Eye, while in the sales meeting and show how it produces Word and Excel documents that can be customized to the target's company.

Feature 2: We can show the internal marketing process that our team developed for Lenovo, which included e-mail flyers, posters, and a Web site, none of which involved any work on the part of the target.

Need: Support (Knowledge)

Feature 1: We can show *Network HR* magazine, which we publish each quarter with training and development articles researched by our own staff.

Feature 2: We can invite the target to send people to our next free training demonstration, where they can network with other HR professionals to gain industry knowledge. We can show the schedule for the rest of the year, proving that we do one event per month.

Need: Convenience

Feature 1: We can demonstrate how our Open Eye system can track multiple training courses in multiple locations around the world.

Feature 2: We can show that we can provide trainers for all areas of development by showing a brochure with our multiple trainers, each with different skills.

Need: Scope of Service Area

Feature 1: We can show the addresses of our offices across China and can provide phone numbers for each office.

Feature 2: Here's a referral to another company that can confirm that we trained its staff in non-mainland Chinese cities including Hong Kong and Taipei, as well as in Seoul.

Need: Control

Feature 1: All materials used in training can be cleared with the target prior to the training.

Feature 2: We can give the target full control over the learning management system for the company, essentially allowing them to take over the distribution of trainee reports.

Need: Experience

Feature 1: I can show this book as evidence that I know what I am talking about. I'll even have a photo on the jacket to confirm that I'm the author.

Feature 2: My whole sales staff can show newspaper clippings from *Shanghai Daily* and *Beijing Today* newspapers, as well as *Eurobiz* and *Network HR* magazines, all of which are published in China.

Need: Speed

Feature 1: We can show that we have materials already developed for the training topic requested.

Feature 2: We can also see all of our trainers' calendars in real time and so can confirm the availability of the proposed trainer within the meeting.

USING THE FEATURES FOLDER

Once you have created a features folder, you need to keep it up-to-date. At sales meetings, allocate time for your team to share the contents of their folders and make photocopies for others, if necessary. You may also want to conduct a "which feature goes with which need" test, like the ones my previous boss, Michelle, used to conduct.

Regardless of whether you conduct formal tests or not, ensure that your team can quickly present the correct correlating feature during a sales meeting.

And remember, as Aldous Huxley said, facts have little meaning if used without thought. If the target cares little about the size of your company, but rather has a need for speed of delivery or flexible payment terms, then you will be talking nonsense if you introduce size as a feature in a sales meeting. Matching the right feature with the target's need is paramount, as it leads to a benefit.

CHAPTER 4

Benefits

*You will not be satisfied unless you are contributing something to or
for the benefit of others.*

—Walter Annenberg (1908–2002)

S o what exactly is a benefit? Ask yourself, "Will I be better off with
this product or service?" If the answer is yes, then there is a benefit for you. To paraphrase the late billionaire Walter Annenberg,
you won't satisfy your sales targets if your target doesn't see a benefit.
You need to match the subjective needs of the target with your company's objective features to complete the target acquisition equation
shown at the beginning of Chapter 1.

Commit this equation to memory, and if you manage a sales team,
then write it on the wall. Salespeople who forget this equation ultimately fail. They revert to "pitching" the target their company's features, which are more often or not irrelevant—just like Huxley's
ventriloquist's dummy talking gibberish.

LINKING TO BENEFITS

That isn't to say that if you know this equation you'll find it easy to
link the target's need to your feature smoothly. It takes practice to find
the right words, and once again, I've used my own business as an
example. The following sections present sentences that should give
you an idea of the tone to use:

Need: Risk Aversion

Linking sentence 1: I also agree that you can never be too careful these days. Always best to use the best, I always say. With that said, I'm sure you know that we were awarded "Training Firm of the Year" at the annual CCH China Staff Awards in Greater China for two years in row.

Linking sentence 2: As you told me today, you were dissatisfied with your last supplier, and so I'm happy to confirm that our general manager will personally be involved with this project.

Need: Support (Process)

Linking sentence 1: Congratulations on being promoted to training manager. Your company's really growing quickly and it sounds like you will have your hands full. I'd like to remind you that we can automate all of your training and give you a password to our learning management system, which we call "Open Eye."

Linking sentence 2: You are probably already aware that we have a dedicated account manager who will work with you.

Need: Support (Knowledge)

Linking sentence 1: I'd like to invite you to our next demo event—on the 19th of this month. You'll be able to network with between 60 and 80 HR professionals.

Linking sentence 2: Here's the latest issue of our company's magazine, *Network HR*. You can see on page 24 there is a section on creating a "needs analysis" survey for your staff.

Need: Convenience

Linking sentence 1: If you have a few minutes, I can demonstrate our learning management system, called "Open Eye," and show you how you can manage your entire company's training from your computer.

Linking sentence 2: I'm sure you'll be happy to learn that we have multiple trainers who can help you with multiple courses. Take the topic of business etiquette, for example. I've got a copy of Andy Clark's new book, *The World Is Yours*, that I can leave with you."

Need: Scope of Service Area

Linking sentence 1: It's great to hear that your company is expanding into Suzhou. On page 16 of our magazine I have a picture of Mike, who is our Suzhou manager.

Linking sentence 2: You mentioned that you have to manage three offices—Beijing, Shanghai, and Shenzhen. I'd like to show you the program that we created for a company similar to yours in those three cities."

Need: Control

Linking sentence 1: Our magazine has a "People" section that features interviews with HR experts. I'd like to recommend you for the next issue, if you don't mind.

Linking sentence 2: At the end of this meeting I'll give you an exclusive password for accessing the learning management system for your company.

Need: Experience

Linking sentence 1: I'd like to leave you with this free copy of *Selling Big to China* for you to review. I've written it based on more than 15 years of sales and negotiations experience, particularly here in China.

Linking sentence 2: The trainer who conducts the "Intensive Business Writing" course is Eugene. Here's a newspaper clipping from the *Beijing Today* newspaper, where he discusses one of his techniques.

Need: Speed

Linking sentence 1: As you mentioned, you need the training next Friday. I'm happy to say that our staff are all full-time, and so we can reshuffle their schedules and make sure we can provide the training.

Linking sentence 2: Yes, two weeks' notice is rather short, but we have a virtual library of our material that all of our trainers share, so although your course will be customized, I can pull it together within two or three days."

USING THE LINKS

Once you verbalize the link between your target's need and your feature, you must substantiate your feature with evidence. It is only at this point in the sales meeting that you will open your features folder and begin selling in the traditional sense. As much as 30 or 45 minutes may have passed from your initial handshake to this point. I discuss the process that follows in Part Two of the book, but here's an illustration of how the first part of the TAE works in practice:

Anna is in the middle of her annual performance review with her boss, Mike.

"Mike, I'd like a raise, and I think a thousand dollars is appropriate," says Anna.

"Anna," Mike replies, "You have done a great job this year, but the company has suffered significantly from the global financial crisis. I would love to give you a thousand dollars, but I just can't. Business is tough at the moment. Unfortunately, that's my final decision."

"This is not fair. I don't think this company acknowledges the contributions I've made this past year," says Anna.

"My hands are tied on the raise. I'm sorry," replies Mike.

From this dialogue can you identify what Anna's needs are? If you said "US$1,000" then you are wrong. This is her want. If you said "recognition," well done. This need was indicated by her expression, "I don't think this company acknowledges the contributions I've made this past year."

And what are Mike's needs? His job as manager requires him to maintain the company's stability. Paying a US$1,000 raise runs counter to this need, given the financial crisis and his company's current poor cash flow. If he doesn't give her the raise, Anna will be angry and might quit, which could affect his company's business. If he pays her the raise, he could lose his job. This is a classic case of a win-lose situation because it is based on positional negotiations and not needs-based negotiations.

However, if Mike identifies that Anna's true, and hidden, need is recognition (see Figure 4.1), then he has more than one feature to match her need. He can show recognition inexpensively by using resources already available. After conducting a quick features audit, he

FIGURE 4.1 Matching Features to Needs

will discover that his company has an empty corner office, a spare seat in a management training program, the ability to add holidays to staff contracts, a space in a new coaching program where the GM personally works with high-potential staff, and a vacancy for a staff member to attend an international conference in Japan next month. Of course, he doesn't disclose them all at once.

Instead, he says, "We definitely appreciate you, and I would like to show you the recognition you deserve. We also think you had a great year, and want to keep you satisfied. While we aren't in a position to offer you a thousand-dollar raise, I can offer you Zhou Li's old corner office. The one with the river view."

"Oh, really? The one next to the general manager? That would be great! But . . . "

" . . . and we would like to offer you a position in the high-potential coaching program. The general manager would personally be working with you and two others. What do you say?" adds Mike.

And if that doesn't work, Mike can offer one of the other features he had identified from his features audit. The more features you can identify the more likely you are to find a way to meet the other's needs and therefore create a benefit.

I like to compare this first part of the TAE to getting to participate in the Olympic Games. First you must be chosen by your home-country selectors. They have the need, say, of having a runner faster than 14 seconds in the 110-meter hurdles. You hold the feature of qualifying in a recent sports meet at 13.67 seconds. You've met their needs, and so the selectors see a benefit in choosing you to compete on behalf of your country. However, being selected only means that you will compete. It does not mean you will necessarily win the gold medal. This is because on the day of the race you will have competitors who are also vying for this prize. Metaphorically speaking, this gold medal is a signed contract. To win the gold medal, you have to be faster on the day. To be awarded the contract ahead of your competitors, you must have greater trust. This is the second part of the target acquisition equation:

$$\textbf{Goodwill} + \textbf{Reputation} = \textbf{Trust}$$

The next three chapters take up each part of the TAE in turn.

CHAPTER **5**

Goodwill

I make every customer want to do business with me. From the moment he walks in, I don't care if I haven't seen him for five years, I make him feel like I saw him yesterday, and I really missed him.

—Joe Girard (1928–)

Goodwill encompasses rapport and friendship. Building goodwill ensures that the target feels comfortable with you, and because everyone prefers to buy from friends, this increases your chance of arriving at a signed contract. I believe that the best Chinese translation for goodwill is 好人缘 (*hǎo rén yuán*). Joe Girard would agree to the importance of goodwill in a sale and negotiation. He is rated in *Guinness World Records* as the world's most successful salesman, selling 13,001 cars at a Chevrolet dealership between 1963 and 1978, and from the quote that opens this chapter, it would appear that goodwill played a major part in his success. But does a lack of goodwill damage business?

Back in June 2007 I happened to be in Hong Kong on a business trip and so decided to upgrade my mobile phone, as I knew the prices would be better than in mainland China. If you've shopped in Hong Kong, you know that Nathan Road, in Kowloon, is a popular street for electronic goods. You probably also know that it can be a tourist trap where unscrupulous salesmen convince tourists to pay for features that they don't need. However, for the seasoned negotiator there are plenty of good deals, because of the many shops competing for business.

Prior to my trip, I had already settled on the phone that I wanted—the HTC Touch. Research trips in Shanghai had earlier confirmed that its features—especially its ability to synchronize with my laptop's calendar and contacts list—matched my needs, saving time and being organized. These needs had developed from being constantly asked by my sales team, often when I was on the move, if I was available for meetings or trainings on certain dates. I was annoyed at having to power-up my laptop each time to review my calendar before giving an answer. The HTC Touch had the benefit, that is, I'd be better off with it. Who I bought the phone from, however, was undecided.

As I already mentioned, Nathan Road has many electronics stores, all vying for business, and so the second part of the TAE came into effect:

Goodwill + Reputation = Trust

Who I bought the phone from was now completely dependent on the level of trust. The first shop that I approached stocked the Touch, and the price seemed reasonable.

"I'd like to look at this model," I said, pointing at the phone through the glass display table.

The salesman, in his 30s and sporting a ponytail, grabbed it out and placed it in front of me. It was clear from his body language and facial expression that he considered me only as a curious tourist, not a potential customer.

"This phone is made in Nanjing," I said, somewhat between a question and a statement.

"No." He answered bluntly. "Taiwan." He returned to the conversation with his colleague.

"Sorry?" I said. I was a little annoyed at his nonchalant attitude, and I was sure the phone was made in Nanjing. In fact, I began to recall a train journey from Shanghai to Nanjing that had happened about a year earlier. A passenger had leaned over, after noticing that I was using an earlier HTC model, and introduced himself as David, the GM of Dopod; HTC's sub-brand in mainland China. He had even gone as far to invite me to his showroom in Nanjing to show the more updated models. So, yes, HTC was made in Nanjing. I was sure of it!

"It's not made in Nanjing," said Mr. Ponytail. Now he did nothing to hide his disinterest with our conversation.

"Really, because—" But I never got a chance to finish my sentence.

"OK, it's made in Nanjing. You are right," he said sarcastically, cutting me off mid-sentence. I think he even rolled his eyes.

"Wow," I thought. "This guy doesn't realize what he has just lost!"

"Thanks. Good-bye," I said, finishing our conversation. There was no way now that I was going to give my money to this man. I turned on my heel and walked into the very next shop, where I bought their HTC Touch. Before I handed over my money, I took the back off the phone and laughed. There, in plain English, were three words. "Made in Taiwan."

In this example, the second shop won by default. Their goodwill was zero, but that was more than the first shop had managed to score. It was in the negatives. But please note, building goodwill is not just limited to your staff in the sales department. It's relevant to procurement as well. Here's the example I give in my training on the subject:

Doing business, whether buying or selling, is a relationship. And, as with all relationships, there is give-and-take. I extrapolate this give-and-take another step and make it mathematical. Imagine, if you will, that "giving" is a positive (+) and "taking," or receiving, is negative (−). Not negative in a you're-a-bad-boy sense, of course, just in a mathematical context. As the old saying goes, "It is better to give than to receive"—and that's why I have linked the "+" symbol to "giving" (providing a product or service) and the "−" symbol to "receiving" (collecting money for it). Ultimately, the process of buying and selling cancels out the positives and negatives. Here's an example.

Say your supplier provides your business with a part, say a silicon chip. This chip is added to your state-of-the-art, hand-held thingamabob, which you then sell to your customer. This movement, from supplier to customer, left to right, is a giving relationship, and therefore a "+."

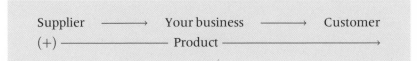

In return, your customer pays your business money (which you receive) for the thingamabob, and you, in turn, pay your supplier for the silicon chip. This is "receiving," and therefore a "−."

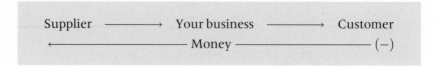

In China, on the 15th day of the eighth lunar month (which is generally around mid-September), many people celebrate the Mid-Autumn Festival (中秋节; *zhōng qiū jié*), also known as the Moon Cake Festival. On this day, suppliers often send moon cakes (月饼; *yuè bǐng*), or vouchers for moon cakes, to their targets to build goodwill, or to use a Chinese expression, to build *Guanxi* (关系). You may have sent moon cakes to your customers for the same reason. This act of giving (+) is also intended to build goodwill.

Supplier ⟶ Your business ⟶ Customer
(+) ———————— Goodwill ————————⟶

And what is the intention of building goodwill? Ultimately to increase business and to make more money, which is again receiving (−).

Supplier ⟶ Your business ⟶ Customer
⟵———————— More money ———————— (−)

This is where most buy-and-sell relationships end. But what would happen if the customer built goodwill with the supplier? What if, on the 15th day of the eighth lunar month the customer sent moon cakes to the supplier instead of the other way round? The give-and-take relationship is turned on its head.

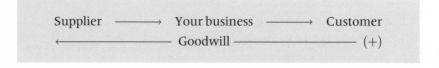

As I mentioned earlier, this relationship can be neutralized. What would the customer receive (−) from this reversed act of goodwill? What could a supplier possibly give a customer in return? Discounts. Better quality. Faster service. Simple.

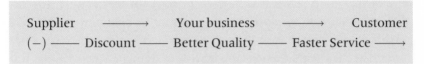

Supplier   ⟶   Your business   ⟶   Customer
(−) ——— Discount ——— Better Quality ——— Faster Service ⟶

That's why this book refers to the other party as a target, not only as a customer. Building goodwill with your suppliers is just as valuable as building goodwill with your customers. As previously mentioned, saving a dollar is more valuable as making a dollar, and therefore both suppliers and customers are targets.

THE POWER OF GOODWILL

And here's an example of just that.

Two years ago I was introduced to a case where a Chinese-owned original equipment manufacturer, based in the southern province of Guangdong, dropped its long-term client, Hewlett-Packard (HP). The HP procurement department was placing what the manufacturer's customer support team thought were unfair demands on its entire supply-chain. Lead-time had dropped from a month to 15 days, and now HP procurement was demanding another significant cut due to the global financial crisis. Didn't they know that the crisis was affecting manufacturers in Shenzhen as well?

According to the company's sales team, HP represented a major share of their entire customer base—approximately 40 percent—and when they first secured the contract the sales team had been very excited. However, each month the demands from HP kept arriving and the sales and customer support teams found themselves spending more and more time solving problems with the HP account, which obviously took time away from developing new business.

HP had used the corporate green card to secure a low price on the initial contract, but it was clearly arrogance and a lack of respect that was hurting the client-supplier relationship once the ink had dried. And then everything changed.

On Monday morning, the HP procurement manager received a phone call and the procurement team was informed that they would have to source a new supplier. HP was caught completely off guard. With no alternative source in hand, HP took months before the shipping of its laptop series was back to normal. In the process, HP lost millions of dollars, because a laptop cannot be sold without a US$2 power cable.

When I teach the power of goodwill to trainees across China, it is clear that while the audience understands the theory, in practice they are quite different, particularly the *Balinghou* and Old Red Guard generations. It is the stick and not the carrot that these generations believe is the most effective, and they regard showing kindness as a sign of weakness. Some even say "it is the Chinese way" to be tough, but then I tell them a story, and everything changes.

A few years ago, my company's Beijing office cleaning lady fell off a bus and broke her leg. This all happened on a Sunday, and we were informed of her misfortune on the Monday morning when we came back to work and found her absent. Mike, the national sales manager, happened to be in the Beijing office and was contemplating paying the poor lady some compensation, to support her over the six weeks that she would be out of work and without salary.

It was while Mike was deciding what to do that we were visited by a rather rude man.

"Hey!" said the man, speaking in Chinese, as he walked into the office and pointed a finger at the receptionist. "I'm not happy!" he shouted. Mike heard the commotion and came striding down the corridor. "My wife had an accident, and now she can't work!" continued the man in a clearly northern Chinese accent.

"Who is this man?" asked Mike, as he approached the receptionist.

"This is the husband of our cleaning lady," replied the receptionist, who was clearly relieved by the arrival of a senior manager.

"What does he want?" continued Mike.

"What do you want?" said the receptionist, as she forwarded on Mike's question.

"Money! I demand compensation!" shouted the husband, clearly using his tone and volume to instill fear. The receptionist translated.

"OK," asked Mike. "How much do you want?"

The husband was quiet for a few seconds, as he realized he had reached the critical part in the negotiation. "Eight hundred RMB! Now." (This was just over US$100.)

Mike surveyed the man. Understandably the husband was upset, as any husband would be given a serious accident, but it had been no fault of anyone in the office, and to lash out at the receptionist like this seemed more than unreasonable. It was simply rude.

"OK," replied Mike, indicating that the receptionist should translate. "Give him his 800 RMB."

The man was visibly surprised when the receptionist began counting out the money from the petty cash till, and walked out the door inches taller. And that is where I pause my story, and ask my audience what they thought.

The response generally supports the Chinese culture of using the stick before the carrot. After all, the audience says, the husband got what he wanted. Right?

Well, technically the husband did get what he wanted. But then rewind the scenario back to when Mike was contemplating compensation, and try asking, "How much was Mike considering as a payment before the angry husband arrived?" Truth be told, Mike had decided to pay more than twice the requested sum, and had the husband walked in with a smile instead of a pointed finger, that's what he would have received. Of course the husband will never know this, and to all his friends, using the stick is clearly the best method to use.

POSITIVE LANGUAGE

Don't think of a blue dog. Really! Don't think of a blue dog. Whatever you do, *do not* think of a blue dog. Now, what are you thinking about? Chances are, you are thinking of a blue dog, right? But I said not to think of a blue dog. So why did you think of a blue dog? This is because you can't control your unconscious mind. It is influenced by words, sounds, smells, and images, which in turn, trigger stored memories and their connected feelings.

Think about the last time you heard a song from your teenage years. Does that song recall memories of crushes, heartbreak, of rebellion or freedom? Do images of specific places or people appear in your head? If so, you have tapped into your unconscious mind.

I was reminded of the power of the unconscious mind back in 1999, when I first traveled across China. It was January, and I found myself in Tiananmen Square in central Beijing with my friend Stuart. The square itself was surrounded by a continuous, blue sheet-metal fence, seven feet tall, surrounding the entire grounds, a result of a scheduled one-year renovation. The timing, "by coincidence," was 10 years after the infamous military incident of June 4, 1989.

Standing in front of the portrait of Mao Zedong, I surveyed the area. Thousands of Chinese, mostly tourists, milled around in groups, taking photos of each other, with the Great Leader in the background. One couple caught my eye. An old peasant man, looking in his 70s although he could have been much younger, was standing with a toddler. The two reminded me of the massive changes China had made in the last 50 years. There stood an old Red Guard and a New Emperor—a nickname given to only-children in China.

I pulled out my camera, and as my finger pressed down to snap a photo, the old man looked down to the toddler.

"*Mei you!*" he said gruffly, indicating that he "did not have" what the toddler was asking for. I assumed the toddler wanted candy.

At once, the boy began to cry. Two Chinese words had caused the young boy to feel pain; not physical but emotional. To the young boy, "*mei you*" (pronounced "may yeow") is a negative. Once said, it means that he is not able to have what he wants, and this causes him to feel unhappy. Other words also cause him to feel unhappy—the ones that mean "no," "impossible," and "can not." Words are extremely powerful to the unconscious mind, especially one belonging to a small child.

Fast forward six years later, to the summer of 2005, and I found myself searching for a cold drink on the streets of Shanghai. I found refuge from the heat and humidity in the Hengshan Road subway station, where I also assumed I would find a small shop selling drinks and snacks. I was right. I spied a small stall near the ticket machine. The middle-aged Chinese woman in charge looked up as I approached.

"*Duibuqi. You bing de bing hong cha, ma?*" I said in Chinese. (Excuse me. Do you have cold ice tea?) She looked at me for a second, and then, with her right arm pushed forward and waving back and forth said, in English, "No! No!" Her facial expression was neutral.

Looking back on the situation I understand what was going through this lady's mind. "There is a foreigner coming up to me now. I don't speak English. Hang on, my daughter taught me some English words. Now, what do you suppose he wants?"

She used the word *no* because she thought that, as a foreigner, I would understand, ignoring that fact that I used Chinese language to ask the initial question. What she didn't realize was the power that the two-letter word and the coordinated hand wave had on my unconscious mind.

Milliseconds after hearing "No! No!" and seeing her negative body language my back tensed. My eyebrows angled and my forehead creased. Most likely my blood pressure and heart rate rose slightly. The result was a negative feeling running through my body. A few seconds later, my conscious mind took control as I reminded myself of the cultural differences and the lady's lack of relationship with the word *no*. For her, it was just a sound. She didn't link this noise to a scolding mother, an angry teammate, or a disappointed teacher. The emotional, unconscious connection was absent.

The lesson from the toddler and the saleswoman are the same. We are all affected by negative language. It controls us, if only for a few seconds or milliseconds. But even milliseconds are enough to recall negative feelings. What's worrying is that many of us still use negative language in the workplace without thinking about it. When someone asks you whether you can finish a report by Wednesday, do you state bluntly, "No. That's impossible. It will take another two days," or do you say, "I can finish the report, and can give it to you on Friday"? Listen to yourself, or reread your e-mail replies. Here are some examples to ponder:

> *Original:* "This is not what I wanted. Make the changes and don't make the same mistakes."
>
> *Positive:* "This is good. I think you can make it even better."
>
> *Original:* "This meal is terrible. I want to speak to the person in charge."
>
> *Positive:* "I'd like to speak to the person in charge as I have a few suggestions."

I am not suggesting that you never use negative language, only that an overuse can cause people to attach unconscious feelings to you that will damage your relationship, or goodwill. Think about your e-mail inbox. Are there any names that you dread to see appear? Thomas, a training specialist who works for Volkswagen in Beijing, told me that some of his local Chinese staff do an about-face when they see one specific German boss walking toward them in the corridor. This German engineer has somehow managed to cause panic in his Chinese colleagues, so much so that their logic is overridden by the creation of a big, scary monster. That is the power of the unconscious mind. It would be worthwhile to take some time to look through your e-mail sent items and consider how you'd feel if you were the recipient instead of the sender.

MIRRORING AND MATCHING

"We like people who are like us." I first came across this expression when I was studying the field of neurolinguistic programming. This expression is also known as the "chameleon effect" and refers to the unconscious attraction toward people who display similarity, whether that be related to nationality, gender, or even body language. Since the 1970s, social science researchers have known that we view people who mimic our body language more favorably than those who don't. What's even more interesting is that this effect holds true for interactions with artificial people as well (Bailenson and Yee 2005).

Stanford University researchers tested subjects who interacted with an artificial man or woman in a virtual reality computer simulation. The artificial computer characters either mimicked the subtle head movements of the participants after a four-second delay or displayed head movements recorded from a previous session with another participant. Results indicated that the artificial characters that mimicked the head movements of the participants were rated as more persuasive and likable than those virtual characters that did not. Of further interest was that only 8 out of 69 participants consciously detected the mimicry. This is because mimicry occurs naturally, between friends, family, and even between total strangers who feel an instant attachment, as in the phenomenon of "love at first sight." In this study on the chameleon effect the research was to be used to improve computer game characters. However, it can also be used to get out of danger.

China celebrates International Workers' Day on May 1; the traditional date for the commemoration of this introduction of the eight-hour workday. Since 1997 Beijing music lovers had been celebrating this five-day public holiday with their own music festival; that was, however, until the Olympics came to town.

The 2008 Beijing Olympics brought with it overzealous restrictions on recreation. Restaurants and bars had to close outdoor patios and beer gardens, nightclubs had to drop the volume, and the yearly three-day Midi Rock Festival, a 12-year tradition, was first canceled and then postponed to October the same year. Unfortunately for many of the international acts, the cancellation was only ordered weeks before the first band was scheduled to take the stage; with nonrefundable plane tickets already bought, these rock-and-rollers found themselves limited to tourism. The more enterprising bars in Beijing sucked up the disappointed bands to play at significantly lower rates, and that was where I found myself too, in May of 2008, drinking beer in a dingy pub with a few friends, and listening to international music that was definitely worth more than the US$7 (50 CNY) cover charge and US$3 (20 CNY) beers.

During one of the band's breaks, I headed outside, beer in hand, to chat with friends who had earlier chosen to escape the cigarette smoke. Some 15 minutes or so later, with a dry glass, I headed back into the bar. That's when I met the drunk.

"Excuse me," I said to the man with his back to me, who was blocking the path to the bar.

"Excuse me," I repeated, this time tapping him lightly on the top of his left shoulder. The man was obviously a foreigner, as I could see strawberry blond hair protruding from under his wooly cap. His jacket reminded me of a Canadian lumberjack. The man turned, slightly too far at first, as he swayed back to adjust his balance. His eyes took a few seconds to focus on me.

"Touch me?" he said, with a strong Glaswegian accent. "Touch me? Did ye fook'n touch me?" He was obviously displeased. To my eye, the pint glass in his hand looked like an ancient weapon used to kill English. My unconscious mind screamed to say "sorry" and back away. But I knew better. I had no doubt that had I chosen this option it would have resulted in Braveheart getting angrier.

"Sorry? Sorry? Ye fook'n sorry, are ye? I'll show ye sorry!" he'd have roared, walloping me in the face with either his fist or his half-empty glass of Tsingtao. Of course, I could be wrong. I doubt that though, because this is what happened. Instead of saying "sorry," I engaged the chameleon effect. I mirrored the drunk's body language and matched his accent and tone.

"Touching ye?" I said in my best Scottish accent, which I had gained from taking classes from Scottish university professors during my MBA program. "I'm not touching ye! I'm playing with ye!"

As I said this, I smiled, and gently patted him down with my palms, like security in an airport. The beer glass had a handle and I spun it around, so it acted like an enormous ring on the outside of my hand. I did this all with a smile.

What happened next was a relief, but also evidence that "we like people who are like us." The Scotsman saw before him a fellow drunk. More important, a *friendly* drunk, and this friendly drunk sounded strangely familiar.

"I like ye, mate!" he said to me. A smile appeared on his face. "C'mon, I'll buy ye a drink."

He bought me a drink, and then slid down the bar sideways, finally crashing to the ground. His night was finished. That's how mirroring and matching can work on a Saturday night, but how about in sales?

Claudia, my colleague in Beijing, and I went to meet Gina from British American Tobacco. While Claudia had met Gina on a number of occasions, this was my first visit, and from Gina's body language I could tell that she wasn't comfortable. I was new to her, and we were speaking in my native language, English, not her's, Chinese. From the outset, I began to mirror her, hoping that in doing so I would make her more comfortable and therefore build goodwill. What I didn't expect was that my colleague, Claudia, would unconsciously try to break rapport with Gina by exhibiting an "anti-mirror" posture. Gina was leaning back, but Claudia was leaning forward, meanwhile I looked on and hoped Claudia would realize that she was building a wall between her and her target. But, to my surprise, Gina didn't let that happen. Her unconscious reaction was to mirror Claudia in response. Claudia had unintentionally but successfully *paced* and then *led* Gina.

Pacing-and-leading is a simple test to measure your level of comfort with another person. At first you mirror and match the subject by replicating their body posture while at the same time copying their tone of voice and the words they use. After a few minutes, you then change both, but slowly. If they are leaning back, as was the case with Gina, you lean forward. If they are talking softly, you slowly raise your volume. In the world of neurolinguistic programming you have first paced and then led your subject. If you have built enough rapport with the subject, this will successfully reverse the relationship. The mirrored becomes the mirrorer, if there is such a word, and you have proven that this person is comfortable in your presence.

The sheer fact that Claudia had paced and led Gina into mirroring her own posture told me that Gina was comfortable with Claudia. Their mutual goodwill was extremely high. To Claudia and Gina it was only visible on an unconscious level, but it was completely visible to me. I, of course, continued my conscious mirroring and so by the end of the meeting, we were all leaning forward, elbows on the desk, waving our hands around as we explained our concepts. Claudia may have had no idea, but that didn't matter. The contract was signed and there was no need to negotiate on price.

ADDING GOODWILL IN WRITING

Building goodwill is not limited to face-to-face interaction. It can also be added to your written correspondence. At the end of business communication I often add a line, such as:

"By the way, I heard that you went to Thailand during the Spring Festival break. I trust you had an enjoyable vacation," or "I believe that next week is your birthday. Happy birthday in advance."

Adding this kind of simple sentence before signing off makes your target or KII (key internal influencers) feel special, because you show that you are thinking about them, and this builds goodwill. A word of warning, though. You have to be accurate with your well wishes, or they backfire. In November 2008 I received an e-mail from Judy, a customer my company had assisted a few months earlier. While she understood the value of building goodwill with suppliers, she mistook the U.S. Thanksgiving festival for an international Western holiday like Christmas.

Dear leaders, peers, partners and friends,
Today is Thanksgiving Day! By taking this opportunity, I'd like to express my sincere gratitude for all your care, understanding and support for me and my team across the year. Without your support, we couldn't have made such good achievements this year. We feel very fortunate to have worked with you. And we look forward to your further cooperation!

Best regards,
Judy

I appreciated her intentions, but she confused me for an American (I'm an Australian, by the way), and therefore her e-mail undercut her praise. The equivalent would be for me to wish her a "happy Hanami" in April, which is the Japanese Cherry Blossom Festival. For the record, I replied to Judy's initial goodwill letter and informed her that Australians celebrate Australia Day on January 26, ANZAC Day on April 25, and the Melbourne Cup horse race on the first Tuesday of November. If you know any Australians, you can definitely build your goodwill by mentioning these three days.

"But why include the goodwill at the end of the e-mail? What about adding it at the beginning?" you may be wondering. Here's an example of that:

Dear Wangwei,
James informed me that you were recently promoted to deputy manager. Congratulations.
By the way, I would like to know if you are interested in buying more widgets.

When goodwill is placed at the beginning of the e-mail, before the request, it adds suspicion to the intent of the e-mail, suggesting that you are only being friendly to get something in return. Best to add your goodwill at the end.

RECIPROCATION

Don't be in *Guanxi* debt. As mentioned earlier, *Guanxi* evokes the mantra, "It's not what you know but who you know," in a simple two-syllable word. Strangely, while Chinese use this word almost daily (for example, *"mei guanxi"* means "not at all"; a reply to a compliment) few actually work on developing their own *Guanxi*. Some may even think it is heaven-sent. But *Guanxi* can definitely be self-developed.

Take me, for example. When I decided to move to Shanghai in 2001 I had as much *Guanxi* as a single phone number scribbled in my daily organizer is worth; that is, zero, zip. I also had less than US$4,000 to my name, having spent another US$15,000 traveling around the world for nine months on what I called my "Australian Tour of Duty." Both my parents had done it, and so it was in my blood. That phone number in my mobile belonged to the school that had accepted me, via the Internet, to work as an English teacher. I was 25 years old, and I'd vowed that I'd last six months on that job. Even if it killed me! I only lasted three.

But that was not a problem. I lasted three months with the school because I began developing my *Guanxi* and creating new opportunities. Within a few weeks of arriving in China, I realized that I was vastly underpaid, and so started to look at other opportunities. Shortly after that, I started my own business with a fellow teacher, Andy Clark, and the result was "ClarkMorgan." In the process, unknowingly, we both began to build our *Guanxi* piggybank. It was never done in a conscious way. Rather, we just liked helping out our new friends, as, like us, they were also entrepreneurs. Sometimes we even held *Guanxi* credit with the well-connected.

I had met John (not his real name) via a mutual friend early in 2004. Back then, all I could remember was that he worked in media. Some months later I bumped into him again at a bar in Shanghai, where we started chatting, and I learned that he worked for the *Shanghai Daily*, an English-language newspaper. He noticed that I was a little down in the dumps and asked about it, and I told him I had just had a big fight with my girlfriend. I'd bought tickets for the Shanghai F1 final the next day, and the fight meant I now had an extra ticket. Whether it was the martinis or an unconscious desire to obtain *Guanxi*, I forced

John to take this ticket and join me and my friends the next day. He did, and we had a great time. The ticket had cost me US$120, which would have gone to waste, had I not given it away to John.

Two years later, John returned the favor. The *Shanghai Daily* was looking at new ideas to generate revenue, and John suggested promoting training events and then sharing the proceeds. In fact, he knew just the right partner for the venture—me. Two years after my initial *Guanxi* investment of that otherwise-lost US$120, John returned the favor in the form of more than US$34,000 worth of back-page advertisements in his newspaper. My company's brand exposure boomed, proving the Chinese proverb, "A drop of water shall be returned with the burst of a spring."

To learn more about the power of reciprocation, I recommend reading Robert Cialdini's *Influence: The Psychology of Persuasion*, first published in 1998. You can visit his Web site at www.influenceatwork.com.

COMFORT AND CONFIDENCE LINK

Have you ever walked in late to a dinner party to find that everyone is laughing with the host, and you don't seem to know anybody? The host is so comfortable, and you are the complete opposite. You take a seat and try to disappear.

You can make your target feel equally uncomfortable if you are too slick at a sales meeting. Being comfortable is directly linked with being confident. Decrease either and it affects the other. Think about it, it's simply common sense. However, that doesn't stop many salespeople from trying to look smarter in the sales meeting than the target. Some even go as far as to belittle the very person who will sign the contract, thinking that it somehow makes them appear more like an expert. It doesn't. It reduces your target's confidence and hands the contract to your competitor.

I've found that when I make mistakes in a sales meeting, the pressure is lifted off everyone. I'm not suggesting that you impersonate actor Jim Carey and fall over during the meeting, but forgetting your pen and asking your target if they have a spare, or just asking for help to connect your laptop to the projector, goes a long way in creating comfort. (As long as you're not selling pens or projectors.) Targets unconsciously acknowledge that you are "just human" and this increases their confidence a notch. In turn, their comfort level increases, and goodwill is developed. Humility wins the day.

CHAPTER **6**

Reputation

Our reputation is more important than the last hundred million dollars.

—Rupert Murdoch (1931–)

A company's reputation is its brand. Brands are built via marketing and word of mouth, and as Rupert Murdoch says, a reputation is worth more than a fortune in money. However, while marketing activities are important in building this reputation that kind of message is obviously biased. It is *your* business that is spending money to promote *your* product or service over that of your competitors. This isn't to say that a big marketing budget is a bad thing. Companies with big pockets definitely have an easier time launching new products or services, but maintaining that reputation takes more than money. For long-term success reputation must be built via word of mouth, from *key opinion leaders* (KOLs) and *key internal influencers* (KIIs).

KEY OPINION LEADERS

In the multibillion-dollar pharmaceutical industry, the term *KOL* is used to describe the senior doctors who help companies sell drugs by publicly promoting their choice of medicines to their peers. This influence could be as passive as lunchtime conversations with fellow doctors, or as obvious as conducting formal presentations on behalf of the pharmaceutical company. I know this, because as a drug rep for Hoechst Marion Roussel, which underwent further mergers into Sanofi-Aventis, I often asked KOLs to speak on behalf of my company at various company-sponsored events. While the media occasionally reports that KOLs are often "bought" via cash incentives or holiday packages, I can honestly say that the only kickback I gave my KOLs was a nice bottle of Australian wine. KOLs are simply the "cool kids" at school who initiate the cyclic yo-yo craze.

KOLs can also be entire organizations. If HP, Microsoft, or Coca-Cola began buying your service or product, this decision could influence other companies to follow suit. For this reason, Fortune 500 or Global 100 companies are sought after as their signature on a contract can trigger a cascade of new customers. Many fashion magazines, particularly those that are new, display luxury brand advertisements for free to encourage other, lesser-known brands to copy with paid advertisements. For this reason a smart negotiator can persuade a supplier to drop its prices based on the knowledge that the supplier's need is to gain a KOL to help build a reputation among other potential targets.

When my business secured Morgan Stanley as a customer in 2008, its competitor Merrill Lynch suddenly showed interest in using our services. Morgan Stanley had done its due diligence, paid money for our service, and, what was more important, returned for repeat business. The level of risk for Merrill Lynch was considerably lower, and that made working with us considerably more attractive. Furthermore, experience with Morgan Stanley ensured that that our business understood the financial sector, again reducing the risk of using our service. If only Merrill Lynch hadn't collapsed during the global financial crisis, I'm sure I would have secured that sale!

Many companies also use corporate KOLs in their marketing. Back in 2004, when I was in Japan, I saw an advertisement for SAP in the Tokyo subway.

"Tumi Runs SAP," read the billboard.

This advertisement caught my attention for two reasons. First, Tumi is a large, respected American company that manufactures suitcases and bags for travel and whose purchase of SAP services will obviously influence smaller companies attempting to replicate Tumi's success. The second was the advertisement's implication of diarrhea— as in "tummy runs." Yes, I have a warped sense of humor.

My company maintains KOLs in China. One such opinion leader is Larry Wang from Wang & Li Resources. His company, a recruitment and executive search company, was awarded the title of "Recruitment Firm of the Year" at the China Staff Awards in 2008, beating international competitors including MRI Recruitment. Larry has personally written two books on the development of staff within organizations in China and is regularly asked to speak in front of HR managers across China. In essence, he is a leading expert in the field of human resources. So when Larry says that he admires ClarkMorgan in public and highlights our success, people listen. I know this because I'm often part of the same audience. At the 2009 "TalentPole" conference in Shanghai on retention and rewards, Larry took a moment to cast the spotlight on my business for a few seconds, informing 60 senior HR professionals of our own achievements in the field of training and development. Of course, I could have boasted about receiving the "Training Firm of the Year" award two years in a row, but it would have sounded like blatant and arrogant self-promotion. When a KOL says it, it becomes unbiased and credible.

The charity 51SIM goes one better than that with its KOL: former U.S. President Bill Clinton. The organization, which promotes what it calls a "sustainable innovation movement" in China, features a video of Clinton thanking 51SIM's co-founder, Daniel Foa, and praising the work done by the charity in China. The former president then hands Daniel a certificate of appreciation from his own charity, the Clinton Foundation. The value of Clinton's endorsement to the reputation of 51SIM is obvious. Nevertheless, your own "Larry" is also valuable.

WOMBAT SELLING

This value comes from contracts directly linked to your KOLs' endorsements. Because KOLs influence others to buy, it is of strategic importance to get your KOLs and targets together in the same room, talking to each other, as often as possible. Hewitt-Gleeson introduced the acronym I've used for the heading of this section in his 2006 book,

WOMBAT Selling. WOMBAT selling, or Word Of Mouth, Buy And Tell, is a catchier way of saying "referral," which is why your sales team will remember it. Here's an example of WOMBAT sales:

Back in 2007 I bought an HTC Touch mobile phone. I never saw any advertising, nor was I approached by sales staff. Rather, my colleague Sheldon had one resting on his desk one afternoon. It was a cool-looking phone with a large screen, and it predated the Apple iPhone's launch by almost a year. I asked Sheldon what he thought of his high-tech-looking mobile, and his enthusiasm and excitement caught my attention. Within two weeks I had bought my own. WOMBAT sale number one. Some two months later, another colleague, Nigel, saw me playing with my HTC phone. After he asked, I responded that I loved it—and a week later he was WOMBAT sale number two.

WOMBAT sales take no energy on our part. In fact, we do it all the time without thinking, by boasting about our favorite hairdresser, restaurant, or movie. We also do it less obviously by wearing their brands on our body. So how do you promote WOMBAT sales in your organization? You follow our lead.

My company went from a virtual unknown in 2002 to its first "Training Firm of the Year" award in 2007, only five years later. Part of our success was linked to WOMBAT selling. From early 2006 to late 2008 our marketing team arranged monthly networking events in bars and restaurants. They also arranged monthly training demonstrations in five-star hotels and business centers, a practice we continue to this day. For this three-year period, we maintained eight offices, which meant we were creating as many as 16 WOMBAT sales opportunities each month. Each event would attract as many as 120 participants, a group made up of about 25 percent current targets and 75 percent potential targets. This equated to an opportunity of WOMBAT selling to more than 1,400 targets a month, or 16,800 per year.

One such WOMBAT selling event that sticks in my mind was held in August 2008. Andy, the events manager, secured Sugar, a dessert restaurant and bar in the upscale Xintiandi bar and restaurant district in Shanghai. The space had an official capacity of 60, but on the night over 80 people attended. Again, there was a similar

1:3 ratio of current targets to potential targets, and the mood was perfect for networking. As the participants made candy animals from sugar-based dough, my sales team wandered between the groups, introducing new faces to regular clients. KOLs from SAP, BHP Billiton, Morgan Stanley, and Li & Fung were casually introduced to the targets in a fun and relaxed atmosphere. All our sales team had to do was play host while our KOLs conducted WOMBAT selling on our behalf. As mentioned earlier, a boast always sounds better coming from a happy customer than it does from your own mouth, and our KOLs were doing a great job building our reputation. The return on investment for that event was approximately a multiple of 50.

KEY INTERNAL INFLUENCERS

Although getting in front of a target is a major goal in business, sometimes these important people are too busy, or simply don't want to see you, no matter how impressive you think your product or service is. This is where your key internal influencer, or KII, steps in.

As I mentioned earlier, Miller and Heiman define four kinds of individuals they call "Buying Influences," that is, the "Economic Buying Influencer," the "User Buyer Influencer," the "Technical Buying Influencer," and the "Coach." This forth type, the Coach, differs from the other three in that this role is supportive. Rather than interfering with your sale, Coaches add weight to your message, and because they are independent from your business, they can be far more persuasive than any of your company information found on your brochure, Web site, or within a DVD. This "Coach" is a key internal influencer (KII); another synonym in the sales and negotiation book of jargon. There is, however, a difference between the Miller and Heiman "Coach" and my KII. More often than not, KIIs don't realize that they are representing your best interest back in their workplace. Coaches are always aware of their support.

A KII could be your target's receptionist, assistant, or colleague. Regardless of their position in the target's company, their opinion is highly valued by the target, and hence they can aid in building your company's reputation. During the Clinton presidency, Hillary Clinton was wooed by numerous lobbies, charities, and organizations due to her closeness to the president. These groups tried to get their message included in "presidential pillow talk." Here's a joke to further my point:

> During Bill Clinton's presidency, Bill and Hillary decided to go for a drive to see the countryside. Suddenly Bill, who was driving, realized he was almost out of gas. He pulled into a tiny gas station where a man walked out of the store to help them.
>
> Hillary looked up and screamed with obvious glee.
>
> "Harvey! Is that you? I can't believe it!" Hillary jumped out of the car and gave the man a big hug. Bill watched as they proceeded to talk for a number of minutes.
>
> When they were finished talking Hillary returned to the car.
>
> "Honey, who was that?" asked Bill.
>
> "That was Harvey, an old boyfriend of mine," she responded. "We dated for a long time, and almost got married."
>
> "Wow, just think," said Bill. "If you had married him, today you would be the wife of a gas station attendant."
>
> "No," said Hillary bluntly, "Today Harvey would be the president of the United States!"

The key is not to ignore the KIIs. They can often be linked directly to the success of your target or, at the very least, offer advice to the target when decisions are difficult. They are also generally easier to approach than the target because they are often less busy, or are more accessible after working hours.

Many of the attendees of my company's WOMBAT selling events are actually KIIs. Their bosses, our actual targets, are apt to be too busy to attend such events, and so—knowing this—we aim to impress their junior colleagues. These colleagues generally do not have family commitments that prevent them from attending evening events. However, they are no less important. When we ran an event in each of our eight cities, we ensured that we saw hundreds of KIIs a month. The next day, in hundreds of tea and coffee rooms across China, those attending KIIs would WOMBAT sell my company to their elusive bosses, the targets. This indirect method of getting to decision makers has proven financially rewarding for my business, and is almost completely ignored by my competitors.

Once you are familiar with goodwill and reputation, you can begin to assess the level of trust a target holds for your company.

CHAPTER 7

Trust

Without trust, words become the hollow sound of a wooden gong.
With trust, words become life itself.
—John Harold Hewitt (1907–1987)

The combination of goodwill and reputation creates trust with your target. It is trust that makes us buy; whether that's buying an idea, a product, or a person for who they are. Without trust a sale and successful negotiation on price is nearly impossible. And once trust decreases, a competitor can step in.

My business had been training Nortel Communications for almost four years. The first account manager, Serena, had built strong goodwill with Sandy since December 2005, but it wasn't until May 2006 that Sandy awarded us a contract. The floodgates then opened. Once the first contract was signed many followed, and ClarkMorgan soon became Nortel's "business partner," as our slogan used to read back then. When Serena left ClarkMorgan, she handed the management of the Nortel account to Joryi, who maintained the level of goodwill and consequently secured further contracts. But then things changed. Like Serena before him, Joryi left for greener pastures, and handed this "cash cow" account to Vince. To the Guangzhou office, it was a no-brainer. Keep them happy, and they would keep signing contracts.

Unfortunately, Vince forgot the power of goodwill. He relied only on our company's reputation from the years of marketing exposure that ClarkMorgan had built, and the trust level began to fall as the goodwill faded. Within a few months there existed little to no goodwill with Sandy, and competitors began to look more attractive. Soon after, the account that had provided hundreds of thousands of yuan in revenue, and that had promised to provide much more, was lost. A review of the disaster showed that almost all of the communication between Vince and Sandy had been via e-mail, with no effort to build goodwill via face-to-face meetings. The only upside to that story was that Nortel went into Chapter 11 a few months later, and all training was put on hold anyway. Nevertheless, it put a bad taste in my mouth, as Vince should have known better. His mistakes are now paid for by another employer, and everyone in our company understands that reputation alone can not maintain trust.

While the first part of the target acquisition equation (TAE) was absolute, that is, you either met the target's need or not, this second part of the TAE is scalable. This 0–6 scale allots three points for goodwill and another three points for reputation. It is hardly scientific, but it does give you something to gauge rough success. Here's how I break the score down:

Goodwill

0 Points	You have never met the target before. This is essentially a cold call.
1 Point	You have met the target on one occasion at least. This may have been in the office or at an event.
2 Points	You have met the target a number of times and know about the target's family status and interests outside work.
3 Points	The target has called you up before to invite you to dinner or drinks, *and* paid the tab!

Reputation

0 Points	The target has never heard of your company before.
1 Point	The target is aware of your company, but has never used your services before.
2 Points	The target thinks your company is quite well known, but has probably never used your company before, or you

may have worked with a different division from that of the target.

3 Points The target has used your company before and is very familiar with your business. Its people are so satisfied that they are likely to be WOMBAT sellers.

The combination of points from goodwill and reputation will equate to your overall trust score. In a SWOT analysis (strengths, weaknesses, opportunities, threats), your trust score will indicate whether you are in a strong or weak position in relation to a specific target. A combined score of four or less is weakness and could lead to losing business to competitors. It is in your best interest to ensure that both your goodwill and reputation reach the maximum values of three to ensure that you are not threatened by competition. The trust score can also assist you with analyzing your threats.

Imagine that one salesperson is responsible for your company's largest account. Over the past five years, this sales rep has built up a very strong relationship with the target, to a point that when they are talking on the phone, you don't know if your salesperson is talking to a client or a close friend. You're clearly looking at a score of three for goodwill. The fact that your two companies have been doing business for the past five years also suggests that your reputation, in the eyes of the target, is high. Therefore, you sit comfortably in the knowledge that your trust score is six. You are unlikely to lose this business any-time soon. But then your salesperson quits, and three months later your tender with the client is rejected. Your company's largest account goes to competitors. All this after five years! "What happened?" you ask yourself.

Based on the TAE, it is clear that you were able to meet the needs of your target, but when you lost your salesperson, you also lost your goodwill. Your trust score essentially went from six to three overnight. Any competitor with a score of three or above had the opportunity to poach your business. What should you do to avoid this threat?

Make sure that each target has more than one link to your company. This could mean that your sales manager attends sales calls with subordinates from the unit, or that all sales territories overlap. If the primary link is severed through the loss of a sales staff member, then at least your goodwill score doesn't drop to zero. You might not maintain the same score, but you have a platform to build from. I know this because it is exactly what happened in my business early on in its evolution. I found out the hard way, when Effie, a key salesperson, left my business to further her career. It took almost a year to rebuild goodwill with Degussa, while adidas and Philips disappeared altogether. Such is the cost of losing goodwill.

My final note regarding trust in China is to emphasize its relative scarcity, most likely due to the Cultural Revolution. While the concept of community is slowly seeping back into the larger cities, there is still a lot of distrust between individuals. Dutch organizational sociologist Geert Hofstede highlights that China has the lowest "individualism ranking" among Asian countries and that this "collectivism" can manifest in a close and committed member group, be that a family or an extended family (Hofstede 2009). Unfortunately, in my experience, this "member group" rarely extends into the workplace, and is even less likely in the client-vendor relationship. The relatively few Chinese salespeople who have the ability to bridge this gap are pure gold for their employers.

CHAPTER **8**

Agreement

Understanding does not necessarily mean agreement.

—Anonymous

Once you can make the target see a benefit from using your company, and you build up more trust than your competitors have, then you can expect a quick agreement, right? Well, there is one more issue to consider. You might have thought that I disregarded this factor earlier, but it does play its part: price, or rather, *low price*. I've already stated that price is not the most important factor, but it still matters. And it's just before you get agreement that it can rear its ugly head.

The unfortunate reality is that trust can sometimes be negated by a lower price from your competitor, particularly if your trust score is equal or only one point higher. This is because trust is linked to lower risk, and reducing the price of a product or service can also help to serve this perception. I say "perception" to emphasize the point that perception and fact are not always the same thing. Right? A lower price can help swing the contract back to a competitor, and so can the unethical phenomenon of kickbacks. Modern-day business is still shadowed by tales of targets leaning in favor of competitors that offer the right (that is, illegal) incentive. Once again, this is particularly true if the trust score is similar between competitors. In January 2007, the *New York Times* and *International Herald Tribune* reported that 22 people were being investigated by Chinese police in relation to bribery that ensnared seven of the world's biggest companies, including McDonald's, Whirlpool, McKinsey & Co., and ABB. Unlike past cases of corruption that were most commonly linked to bribing government officials, these cases against the multinationals were all in relation to taking kickbacks from government officials to place business in their areas. There is little room for trust when this style of business is practiced, so I suggest giving companies that engage in kickbacks a wide berth. Well, at least until their target is replaced with one that is more ethical.

Unfortunately, it is not unethical for your competitors to undercut you in price, which can affect your chances of reaching an agreement. This is because your final agreement value can be reduced (or increased) by P, or the price quotient. The price quotient (P) is your competitor's price divided by your price.

Price Quotient = Competitor's Price/Your Price

If your price is the same (or very similar) to your competitor's, then the P is equal to one divided by one (that is, $1/1 = 1$). Therefore there is no change to your trust score. However, if your company is twice the price of your competitor, then your overall trust score is divided in half (that is, $1/2 = 0.5$). And finally if your price is half that of your competitor's price, then the price quotient (that is, $1/0.5 = 2$) multiplies your final trust score by two. Here's how these three price quotients affect your overall agreement result:

Scenario 1: Your price is similar to your competitor's ($P = 1/1 = 1$).

Agreement = Benefits (1) + Trust (1 to 6) × Price Quotient (1)

Result = No change to your trust score.

You know that if you divide any number by one then there is no change to the original value. Therefore if you are similarly priced, then there is no effect on your trust level and so you retain the level of agreement. (This is assuming that the competition doesn't bribe your target.)

Conclusion: In Scenario 1, you are most likely to reach an agreement with your target, as long as your trust level is higher than your competitor's.

Scenario 2: Your price is double that of your competitor (P = 1/2 = 0.5).

Agreement = Benefits (1) + Trust (1 to 6) × Price Quotient (1/2)

Result = Your trust level is halved.

In this case your entire trust value has been cut in half, because you are twice as expensive. Few companies are ever that audacious! You can't expect to be twice the price of your competition and not have something else up your sleeve. That "something" has to be lots of trust. That is how plastic surgeons make their money. Goodwill and a lot of reputation make good surgeons very, very rich. And the more reputation they have the more they can charge.

In Scenario 2 you must have a lot more trust than your closest competitor to retain a price twice that of your competitor. If your trust begins to fall, then so should your price, or you will start losing contracts to competitors.

Conclusion: In Scenario 2, you are only going to win if your original trust score is at least twice that of your competitor.

Scenario 3: Your price is half that of your competitor (P = 2/1 = 2).

Agreement = Benefits (1) + Trust (1 to 6) x Price Quotient (0.5)

Result = Your trust score effectively doubles simply because your product is ridiculously cheaper.

If you happen to have more trust than your competitors, you'd be silly to offer half their price. But if you did, you'd essentially be doubling your chances of reaching an agreement. Remember—there is no such thing as a sure thing in negotiations, but in this third example you'd be very, very unlucky if you didn't get the deal. Mind you, you'd be missing out on a lot of profit, and that's not too smart.

Conclusion: In Scenario 3 you would only halve your price if you knew that you had a lot less trust than your competition, say for example, if your company was a new player in the market. But this strategy of competing on price is ultimately doomed, because sometime in the future another new player will arrive in the marketplace and they will use this same strategy against you. The only winner then is the target. Instead of losing money per contract by offering a considerably lower price than your competition, it is wiser to spend that same money on building trust. A 10 percent increase in your marketing and PR budget to increase your company's reputation and consequently your trust score is strategically smarter and less costly than the equivalent in discounts to your target. This is because spending on reputation is seen by all of your targets, whereas a discount to secure a contract is only seen by one target.

To recap the basic theory, needs plus features equal benefits, and goodwill plus reputation equal trust. As important as trust is, a final agreement can be affected by price. That's enough to go on with, and begin to put the equations into practice.

Part Two

The Sales Call

CHAPTER **9**

Checking

Ninety percent of life is just showing up.

—Woody Allen (1935–)

You may be thinking that once you understand the target acquisition equation (TAE), you can go out and get 'em! Well, not so fast, bucko. First the target must want to meet you. And for that to happen, the target has to know you exist. Anyone for chess?

Checking, a verb meaning to remind your target (or KII) of your existence, comes from Michael Hewitt-Gleeson, who first coined the expression in his 1990 book *Newsell*, and he wasn't talking about the sort of checking that involves following up to see if instructions have been followed. He was thinking about the game of chess. In chess, when the king is threatened by an opponent's piece, the king is considered to be "in check." The player has three options at that point: move the king out of harm's way, block the check with another chess piece, or take the opponent's piece that initiated the check. Each choice revolves around ultimately saving the king. If the king can't be saved, that is, if none of these three moves can be performed, then the king is said to be "in checkmate." Game over.

Hewitt-Gleeson creatively linked this metaphor to sales, and in doing so turned the role of the salesperson on its head. As I discussed earlier, the idea that salespeople close deals is a myth. It is the target that says yes or no to a purchase, not the salesperson. Therefore, the most important activity for a salesperson to do is to give targets the opportunity to say yes. Only when they have the opportunity will there be any sale—or checkmate. Strangely, this is rarely the focus of sales and negotiation books.

Targets won't know that you exist unless you first put them into check. A check could be a telephone call, personal visit, e-mail, or fax. In essence, a target who is in check is thinking about you, and therefore has the option of accepting or declining your offer. Ultimately, that offer is to buy your product or service. Without that initial check you have little chance that the target will randomly contact you, unless you have WOMBAT sellers working on your behalf.

The concept of *check* comes into play in relation to another form of selling—recruiting potential social partners. For instance, a very close friend of mine used to live in southern China—Guangzhou, to be precise. Back then he was single, and every three months or so, he would come and visit me in Shanghai. But I wasn't the only one he wanted to meet. When he flew into Hongqiao Airport, his first action after disembarking, even before collecting his bags from the luggage carousel, would be to type the following message into his mobile phone:

"Hi honey, I'm in Shanghai for the week. Want to catch up for dinner?"

He'd then press "send." Simultaneously, across Shanghai, ten mobile phones would announce the arrival of an SMS message. Now, assuming that all ten girls were not at that moment having a dinner party together, and that my friend is reasonably attractive, what is his chance of getting a date in Shanghai that week? One in ten? Three in ten? Five in ten? Regardless of the absolute number, there *is* a chance that he gets a date that week, right? And that chance was created when he checked those ladies from the airport arrivals terminal.

Now, imagine that when my friend disembarks from the plane he decides "Nah! I won't bother" and does not SMS those ten prospects. As he comes to Shanghai infrequently what is the likelihood that any of them will just happen to call him to see if he's in town that weekend? Remember, he only comes to Shanghai four times a year. What are his chances? Zero to none? Most likely.

And that is the same chance that you have in scoring a contract if you don't contact the target in the first place. If people are not thinking of you, then they definitely aren't going to call to buy your product or service. There's no chance for checkmate. Plain obvious, but mostly forgotten. This is the biggest mistake made by salespeople today. The target decides whether or not to buy. But in a somewhat arrogant and naive way many salespeople believe that targets are always thinking of their product or service. Unless you control a monopoly, you have competitors—and these competitors are doing their best (that is, also checking) to get into the forefront of the target's mind. You are not playing alone.

WHAT CONSTITUTES A CHECK?

A check could be a phone call, e-mail, fax, visit, accidental run-in at a conference, or anything that gets the target or KII thinking about you. It could even be a referral from a WOMBAT seller. I am checking you right now with this book. By the end of this sentence you will be thinking about me, Morry Morgan, and I now have a chance of influencing you. Don't think of a blue dog! Aha! I did it again. If I wasn't checking you, you would have very little reason to randomly think of a blue dog. This concept can make a huge difference to sales.

Suppose that on Monday you send an e-mail to your target, say, Ms. Wang. That day she reads your e-mail and during that time, and for a short period after, your name or that of your company is in the front of her mind. If there happened to be a need for your product or service, your name would be recalled easily, and she might give you a call or drop you an e-mail. A check doesn't necessarily have to ask for a sale, it only has to remind the target that you exist; like the SMS messages my friend sent from the airport. Remember—it is the target who closes the deal.

But on Wednesday your competitor makes a phone call to Ms. Wang, intending to build goodwill and find needs, and also to place Ms. Wang in check. Your e-mail is now forgotten, or at least not at the forefront of the target's mind. If a need for your product or service arises, then there is high chance that Ms. Wang will call your competitor first. Of course, she might call you both, and that is where overall trust will determine the outcome.

Because you may no longer be in the front of your target's mind, checking is a continual process of reminding targets of your existence.

As in the game of chess, when you check the king, your opponent has the ability to avoid checkmate. In sales, avoiding checkmate is the equivalent of saying, "No thanks. Not today." It is a rejection. But, as in chess, when your first check doesn't work, you continue with the game, and check again. "No" only means "Not today." Tomorrow is a different day, with new needs and possibly a new target.

Movie stars have agents for the same reason. It doesn't matter how good an actor is. If the director isn't reminded of that actor's availability, then one of the million other talents available could be chosen.

HOW MUCH CHECKING DO I NEED BEFORE I CAN SIGN THE CONTRACT?

There's no magic number for how many checks it takes to secure a contract. It could be one, or it could be over a hundred. My company has a client relationship management (CRM) system that we named "Open Eye." Open Eye has been recording my salespeople's checks since May 2003. It also records the check type, time, and date, and includes an open field to add comments. BHP Billiton took 16 checks before they became our client. Otis Elevator took 18 checks. The record to date has been Maersk Shipping, which took 87 checks! And patience pays off. Maersk has thus far (as I write) bought 28 training courses, with a value of more than US$120,000, or 840,000 CNY.

Michael Hewitt-Gleeson also practices what he preaches. In 2008 my company launched "Premier Events," a brand that brought international experts to China for one- or two-day courses. Michael informed me, after the contract had been signed and sealed, that he had allotted 10 checks in order to secure his speaking engagement. Apparently I had decided to buy his services at check number six. For his efforts, he made US$26,000 (180,000 CNY). Not bad for a week's work of training and six phone calls.

ARE ALL CHECKS EQUAL?

An e-mail is not as effective as a phone call. It is a monologue, lacks tone, and can be skimmed over or deleted without being read at all. An e-mail is a check, but the weakest form. A phone call is better, as it allows for a dialogue with questions that can determine needs. However, phone calls are faceless; you have no way to read body language, which is a major part of reading unspoken messages and building goodwill.

Meeting someone in person is therefore better than phoning. Often this is done at a conference, where you can address the target or KII face-to-face. I call a meeting in public a group check, and while it is far better than an e-mail or phone call, there could be distractions, such as noise and other people interrupting. The target or KII is not 100 percent focused.

The best option is the *private meeting,* most often at the target or KII's office. At the private meeting you can come fully prepared with brochures, samples, audiovisual equipment, and build goodwill far more easily than at a public event. In my company's Open Eye CRM system we award each of the specific checks a different value, as follows:

- E-mail: 1 point
- Snail-mail: 2 points (physical letter, such as a brochure or magazine)
- Phone call out: 5 points
- Phone call in: 7 points (the target or KII calls you)
- Group meeting: 15 points
- Private meeting: 20 points
- Send proposal: 20 points
- Send contract: 50 points

The different checks have different values because this way you can manage your daily activity, and that of your sales staff. In my company each sales staff member has a requirement to maintain a check score of 1,000 points. This needs to be maintained constantly and is calculated over a continuously moving 30-day cycle. For example, if today was April 4, then our CRM system accumulates all of the checks from March 5 to today. This ensures that check scores are not reset each month, which would demotivate sales staff.

E-mails (1 Point)

Anyone would go batty sending 1,000 e-mails a month to maintain 1,000 points, and as previously mentioned, an e-mail is the least memorable check. Ultimately, you want your sales team to arrange face-to-face meetings, so keep the value of e-mails in your CRM system low.

But that doesn't mean the e-mail check is not valid. It might have a low value, but it is a great way to follow up after a phone call out, group meeting, or private meeting. This follow-up e-mail could be in the form of a "Thank you for giving me your time" message, or an invitation to an event. Of course, an invitation is better, because it leads to a future check.

Snail Mail (2 Points)

Even in the era of e-mail, you still sometimes have to send physical information—that is, snail mail—to targets and KIIs. My company publishes and distributes an industry magazine called *Network HR*, and more than 6,500 of our targets and KIIs read the magazine each quarter. The magazine is bilingual and includes articles on HR-related issues such as remuneration and benefits, recruitment, and my company's specific field of training and development. The back cover always includes an advertisement for my company, so when the magazine is casually put down, there's a good chance that our logo may be passively checking the target or KII. Your company brochure can do the same job if you make sure that your company's name or logo is clearly written on both sides—front and back. Anyone walking into the office of a target or KII could also be put into check, should they look down on the desk.

My company gets creative about our snail mail. Instead of sending traditional Christmas cards in December or Moon Cakes (月饼; *yuè bǐng*) in September, we send International Women's Day cards on March 8 and Chinese National Day cards on October 1. Few, if any, of our competitors do the same, which makes our check even more memorable to our target.

Snail mail checks are worth more than e-mail checks because they can linger longer in the mind or on the desk of the target or KII.

However, as a magazine or brochure may move from the in-box to the wastebasket without being opened, it is less reliable than the phone call out.

Phone Call Out (5 Points)

When you call targets or KIIs you have their attention, if only for a brief moment. Therefore the value of the phone call out check is higher than the e-mail and snail mail, because of the reliability of the check. But phone calls are easily forgotten. The memory of a phone call will always dissipate faster than the memory of a face-to-face meeting. Think about your own experiences. If you regularly see and call your parents, which event is stronger in your memory? The phone call or seeing them in person?

Generally a phone call out will precede an e-mail. This is partly because you may not know the proper recipient for your invitation or product information. But how do you get to the target and not get stopped by a gatekeeper or passed on to someone who has no authority? My tip is to use technology. In my business the HR director is the target, but I may not have a name. If I try to reach this officer anyway, it usually goes like this: On my initial phone call out, I say, "I'd like to speak to the HR director." The gatekeeper, probably the receptionist, says, "If you don't know her name, then I can't put you through." My reply that I have an important invitation or document to give the HR director falls on deaf ears. Gatekeepers receive a dozen calls like this a day. And they get paid to block these calls. They want a name, so give them a name. You only need to get past the gatekeeper, so you type something like this into your favorite search engine:

- facebook hr director (company name)
- linkedin hr director (company name)

In these examples, you insert the target's company name between parentheses. You can also add the city or country to narrow the search. The search result should give you a number of names of people who may or may not still work for that company. The only way to know if they are legitimate is to try them on the gatekeeper.

Alternatively, you can omit the job title and only include the department. For example:

■ linkedin hr shanghai (company name)

This should give you a number of names of people working in the same department as your target. Let's say that your search generates the name "Cathy Hong." You call the gatekeeper, and say, "Hi. I'd like to be put through to Cathy. Cathy Hong please." Your tone does not suggest that you are asking for permission. For all the gatekeeper knows you are Cathy's best friend or colleague. When Cathy answers the phone, you act frustrated.

"Oh, sorry, Cathy. The receptionist was meant to put me through to your HR director."

Three things could happen. First, Cathy could apologize on the receptionist's behalf and transfer you through to her boss, the target. Second, she could mention the target's name, such as, "Oh! You're after Ms. Bao?" and then either transfer your call or ask you to call back using another extension number. If it's the latter and you find yourself talking to the receptionist, you now ask for your target by name. Third, she somehow knows what you're up to and redirects you back to the receptionist. To date, this has yet to happen to me; however, if it does I will ask the receptionist to put me through to one of the other names gleaned from my initial Internet search. One way or another, I will get my phone call out check. The only thing stopping me would be lack of perseverance.

In China, it's also advantageous to use English when calling a target via a gatekeeper such as a receptionist. This works well when calling a multinational company, where the English of the office staff is usually far better than the English of the receptionist. Receptionists under pressure are often quick to transfer incoming calls, in case they are from international managers or customers. It's simply not worth the risk to delay such people, so use this to your advantage.

But what do you say to the target when your perseverance finally pays off? Personally, I believe the best "cold call" is an invitation, and the best invitation is to an event where WOMBAT sellers will be present. So, before you make the phone call out, make sure your marketing department is supporting the sales department by arranging events that are attractive to your targets. However, if you don't have an attractive event on the calendar, your goal for a phone call out is to secure a private meeting.

"Hi, Mr. Wilson," you say to your target, after hurdling the gatekeeper. "I've been working with several companies in your field, and would appreciate a chance to learn your concerns so as to improve my service. Could I come and talk to you about this next week?" If that doesn't work, take a step back. Don't force it. Ask for your target's e-mail address so you can e-mail some information. The rule of reciprocity will kick in here. Having rejected you, your target will probably feel obliged to agree to this concession. However, if you get a hang-up instead of an e-mail address, mark a date in your calendar, no more than a month away, for another call. The target could just be having a bad day.

Phone Call In (7 Points)

Cold calls are not always welcome. There's a Filipino-accented lady who calls me consistently each fortnight, trying to get me to move my money offshore somewhere. Needless to say, she's yet to take more than 10 seconds of my time before I announce over her sales pitch, "Thank you very much. Good-bye." But when the voice on the phone turns out to be a target or KII, that's a whole different matter—you know your prospect is interested and isn't going to cut the conversation short. That increase in buy-in is therefore worth more check points—7 rather than the standard 5 for a call out.

However, a phone call in can also damage your reputation. In Chinese, the casual approach to answering the phone often extends into the workplace. *"Wei?!"* (喂) is an acceptable greeting to a friend or family member, but to those unfamiliar with the Chinese language, *Wei?* can sound snooty, bordering on arrogant. While that is a cultural difference between languages, a foreign customer may take it personally. Therefore, I recommend training your Chinese staff to use one of the following patterns:

- *Wei?!* (喂?!) *Ni hao.* (你好.) XYZ Company. 我是 Jerry. (*Wo shi Jerry.*) (Completely in Chinese.)

- *Wei?!* (喂?!) *Ni hao.* (你好.) XYZ Company. This is Jerry. (Mixing Chinese with English.)
- Hello. XYZ Company. This is Jerry. (Completely in English.)

While *Wei?!* on its own might sound standoffish, combining it with the gentler *ni hao* reduces the abruptness of the tone. Adding one's name at the end of the sentence also makes it easier for the caller to recall the recipient's name, since when it is tucked inside a "Hello. This is Jerry speaking," short-term memory seems to focus on the last word, "speaking," rather than the name. Not very useful.

As a sales manager, be sure to call in to your own office occasionally to assess the greetings your team is using. I also suggest printing out the most preferred greeting from the three listed here, and sticking it near each salesperson's phone.

Group Meeting (15 Points)

As mentioned earlier, a group meeting is not as valuable as a private meeting because the target or KII could be distracted. Group meetings occur when you are at an industry conference, and are often a matter of chance rather than a planned situation. Nevertheless, you have the opportunity to be face-to-face with the target or KII, and that's an important check. You can have a dialogue about your product or service, answer some concerns, or arrange a demonstration the following week. Group meetings can work in conjunction with WOMBAT sales when a satisfied target or KII is also present.

As mentioned under WOMBAT sales, my business creates group meeting opportunities in the form of free training demonstrations once a month, in cities across mainland China and Hong Kong. Each event attracts as many as 100 or 150 attendees. The participants might think that they are getting a free lunch, but they're not. They're providing value by putting themselves in check for the three-hour event. And that means my colleagues and I are giving them an opportunity to say yes to our offer.

Private Meeting (20 Points)

A private meeting is one of the best checks there is. For some industries, a private meeting could be on the golf course, but for most, it's in the client's office. Regardless of whether you're on the back nine or in the boardroom, there is a higher chance of checkmate, that is, a sale, when you control the target's full attention. Don't fool yourself—it's still their decision—but you have seriously increased your chances of making a sale when you stand or sit in front of your target.

The other benefit of a private meeting is that you have multiple opportunities to check the target or KII both before and after the face-to-face meeting. A phone call out (5 points) the day before your private meeting (20 points) confirms the appointment, and an e-mail (1 point) the day after thanks the target for taking the time to meet. To support what you said during the meeting, you might also snail mail (2 points) a physical brochure, magazine clipping, or a sample a few days after. All told, a single meeting could result in 28 points, which brings you closer to that monthly goal of 1,000 points. What's more important, it keeps you in the mind of the target or KII longer.

Send Proposal (20 Points)

Sending a proposal is the equivalent for asking your target for the business. The send proposal check generally follows many other checks (as many as 87, my firm has found, as in the case of Maersk Shipping), and it is most likely requested by the target. However, you should also be asking for business, so at the private meeting you should inform the target that you will follow up with a proposal. Ultimately all checks are useless if they don't lead to a proposal and subsequent sale. Sending a proposal is an extremely effective check because it plays on the rule of reciprocation. You've done something for the targets, by taking time to put together a comprehensive document to help them, and now they feel obliged to reply, preferably in the affirmative.

Send Contract (50 Points)

There's no guarantee that your contract will be signed, but once it is sitting in front of someone, it is a huge check move. All it takes from your target is a quick signature—and in China a stamp of the company chop—and you have reached checkmate!

CHECKS IN ACTION

Using the checking method is a great way to manage your sales force. If you haven't heard it before, here is the key management mantra: "If you can't measure, then you can't manage." When you're a manager of a sales team, checking allows you to measure your salespeople's daily activities. It's objective, and therefore there is no confusion about what is expected. You no longer need to listen to "but the market these days is down" or "I didn't call them because I know they won't buy" excuses from underperforming salespeople. Using the check method also maintains morale.

"Did you check the target today?" is much more motivating than "Did you sign the contract today?" Every member of your sales team can check daily. Not everyone can sign a contract daily. I wish a contract a day was possible for my business, *but it ain't,* and it probably isn't for your's, either. So a sales manager who focuses on actual sales ultimately sabotages the entire team. Hewitt-Gleeson calls this "DYSH-ing"; the verb is an acronym for asking your staff, "Did you sell him?" (Or "her," as the case may be.) If you asked this question of each of your salespeople daily, most of the time most of them would have to reply no. After all, selling is not easy—we'd have had to say no 86 times before that first yes with Maersk Shipping. What effect do you think answering no on a daily basis is going to have on the sales force's morale? Soon your sales staff will stop making any phone calls at all, because, as you keep reminding them, they are failures for not signing contracts. Resignations will follow, and existing goodwill will disappear altogether. Your overall trust level will then drop and you'll find it harder to reach sales targets, even though your product and your company reputation haven't changed.

Therefore, instead, of "Did you sign a contract today?" ask your sales force, "Did you check today?" Even better, ask them, "How much did you check your targets today?" By avoiding negative responses you create positive language in the workplace, which in turn motivates your entire team. And because you have given them a monthly target, say 1,000 points, you can measure their performance. Again, *if you can't measure, you can't manage.*

If the members of your sales team think that 1,000 points is too much, then show them the following table, which illustrates a typical month in my business, consisting of a possible seven checks per target or KII.

1. E-mail target or KII with an invitation to a demonstration.	E-mail = 1 point
2. The day before the demonstration, call the target or KII to confirm attendance.	Phone Call Out = 5 points
3. At the demonstration, introduce the target or KII to trainers and other participants (that is, KOLs).	Group meeting = 15 points
4. Follow up with e-mail thanking the target or KII for attending the event.	E-mail = 1 point
5. Make a phone call a week later to ask for a meeting to discuss the demonstration and possible training.	Phone call out = 5 points
6. Meet the client	Private meeting = 20 points
7. Send a proposal	Send proposal = 20 points
Total	67 points

The total score for doing all seven checks is 67 points. Obviously, not all invitations to a demonstration will result in attendance at the demonstration, and that's why each of my salespeople has a database including at least 120 targets. Each salesperson could easily reach 800 or 900 points even without a meeting. If each of your sales team has more than 120 targets, then you should raise their target beyond 1,000 points. Regardless of the quota, make sure you are tough on that number. Unsurprisingly, when the checks begin to drop, so too do the number of signed contracts.

Be warned, though. Focusing on only one type of check, and being inflexible, can lead to serious problems. For example, a five-star European hotel in Beijing has a policy that each day a salesperson must hold four face-to-face meetings with targets. Each morning before 9 o'clock, the sales team meet and outline to the sales director which clients they will be meeting that day. The director records the information, and then at 5:30 p.m. that same day, the sales team meets again for a debrief, at which point they report their success. Under my scoring system, meeting four targets each day would equal 1680 points a month—a fantastic score, and one that would certainly lead to many checkmates. Alas, if only that score were true. In reality, the sales team finds it extremely difficult to get four meetings a day consistently. Obviously some days are harder than others, due to poor weather, upcoming public holidays, or times where targets are often busy, such as the end of the month. The result? The sales team lie to their director in the morning, and lie at the debrief in the afternoon. As private meetings are the only focus of the senior management they are essentially handicapping their sales team into an all-or-nothing scenario. While a phone call out is not as good as a private meeting, it is by far better than no check at all. Unfortunately, this policy has led to reduced sales and reduced morale, and worse, false reporting that moves up the management chain and could influence projections and strategy.

And it gets worse. This sales process is endemic in the entire hospitality industry in China. From Beijing to Shenzhen and to Shanghai in the middle, salespeople are lying to their senior management because they are given no room to maneuver. With only one form of check to apply, the entire process is tainted.

Time for a review: How do you get targets to buy? You first do a check to give them the chance to say yes. If they say no thanks, then there's no need to become discouraged. Instead, a week or two later, you check them again. I like to say in my business that a no is only a "not today." For my friend at the airport, silence or an SMS reply of "sorry, I'm not free this week" was a no, but that didn't stop him from sending an SMS on his next trip to Shanghai. Persistence pays off. He's married now, to one of his Shanghai targets.

A final word on checking for sales managers. Reluctance to check is common among salespeople. You'll know when they have fallen into this state of mind because they will be extremely busy doing everything except checking. They will be reformatting proposals, modifying e-mail signature lines, cleaning up the addresses in your company's CRM system, or simply gossiping in the office. I agree with Jeffrey Gitomer: "Call [that is, check] reluctance is not a problem, it's a symptom." The cause is your failure to have your team believe in the direct relationship between checking and success. At first, this might require you to police the check score, but later, as the success rate rises, it will be self-evident.

If your sales team is hitting the check score but the team members still appear to be avoiding the phones and are never attending meetings, then make sure they're not *brass plating*, a term that I learned from my pharmaceutical sales days. In Australia, doctors traditionally have a brass plate announcing their name and medical qualifications on an outside wall of their clinic. Lazy pharma reps would simply drive past, not stopping, and read the name of the doctor off the wall. They would then record the event as an actual face-to-face meeting in their CRM system. Hence the term *brass plating*. Again, *if you can't measure, you can't manage*, and that also means that you have to manage the input of those measurements.

MOTIVATING YOUR SALES FORCE

While I was writing this book, self-motivated Chinese staff were hard to come by. The irony is that China—with 1.3 billion citizens—has a management shortage. This peculiar situation is reported by international HR firms Manpower and Hewitt. In 2003 Hewitt went as far as reporting that 60 percent of companies included in their "Best Employers in China" survey were suffering from a senior management shortage. In 2006 Manpower announced, "It will still take six to eight years before graduates gain sufficient work experience to ease the current competition for mid-level and senior managers." Today, these conditions still apply.

So why are we in this predicament? I have attributed this shortage of leaders to three factors:

- Lack of life experience
- Poor foresight
- Poor teamwork

As noted, the poor management and leadership skills can be attributed to the spoon-fed education culture, which prepares students to pass tests through rote learning and does not encourage creative thinking or development of leadership skills outside the school system. The sheer volume of homework and preparation to pass the *Gao Kao*, or university entrance exam, makes it nearly impossible to gain life experience working part-time jobs, even on weekends. Consequently, a 23-year-old Chinese graduate may have less work experience than, say, an American or British 16-year-old, who is likely to have had some part-time or summer jobs. As Tobias, a German senior engineer at Suzlong in Beijing, said to me, "The Chinese engineering graduates have great book skills, but low practical experience. They prefer an office job after graduation." In essence, Chinese graduates, specifically the *Balinghou,* are children in comparison to their Western counterparts and consequently require motivation techniques that recognize this handicap.

The second point to consider when managing a Chinese sales force is the relative lack of foresight displayed by the Chinese, which can often extend to the highest levels of government. For example, back in 2001, Shanghai hosted the APEC summit two weeks after the National Day "Golden Week" in October. Incredibly, the local government only gave two weeks' notice to the burgeoning financial hub, Lujiazui, that the main thoroughfares would be shut down for five days, and that all homes along the motorcade routes would be prevented from opening their windows—apparently to minimize the threat of snipers! No doubt, with the world's leaders descending upon Shanghai, including then U.S. President George W. Bush and Russian President Vladimir Putin, plans to ensure their security would have been drafted years in advance. Unfortunately, this is not a isolated case, and nine years on, examples of shortsightedness are still common. Much of the shortsightedness can be attributed to the uncertainty of the economy as true communism has slowly been replaced with unproven market-driven practices. Nevertheless, shortsightedness is endemic in China today, and it is not just limited to new graduates.

The third weakness of the Chinese workforce, particularly among the men, is their relatively poor teamwork skills, compared with other nations. While the women's soccer team is at world championship level, the men's team is the butt of many jokes in China, and the cause of many empty stadiums. Again, schooling can be blamed for forcing a competitive habit onto hundreds of millions of students, rather than helping them learn to collaborate.

The one-man management style is alive today, most likely created by "Leninist-Stalinist-style communist ideology" (Fang and Hall 2003) formed between 1949 and 1978. This high power distance, when combined with the other dominant Chinese cultural values of high uncertainty avoidance and low individualism (Hoefstede 1980, 1991) has meant that Chinese leaders are loath to delegate, and their subordinates are even more reluctant to volunteer. With very little autonomy and responsibility developing in the lower ranks, and with a culture fearful of making mistakes, it is no wonder that self-motivated leaders, particularly in sales departments, are hard to find. Lynda Baird of FCm Travel Solutions puts it more concisely. "Compared to Hong Kong, the talent in Shanghai is average," she says. So how do we get the best out of them?

Short-Term Targets

Applying short-term targets based around quarterly rather than yearly results ensures that your Chinese staff can more easily visualize their goals. It also means that if they fail to meet one quarter's targets, they are not discouraged for the entire year. This doesn't necessarily mean eradicating the end-of-year bonus, often referred to as the "13th month," but rather breaking this large sum into four smaller bonuses. This ensures that staff are not discouraged if they fail to meet one quarter, as they start from scratch again in the next quarter.

Another weakness of the 13th-month bonus is that it perpetuates high staff turnover rates. In a 2001–2008 PRC study, which they presented at a British Chamber of Commerce meeting in Shanghai, Hewitt reported that staff turnover for all companies was 17.9 percent on average, but in hi-tech it was as high as 29.4 percent, and in retail 26.2 percent. These findings were supported by anecdotal evidence from the marketing director of an American pharmaceutical company based in Shanghai, who complained to me that her sales force turnover was as high as 30 percent. And this was during the global financial crisis, when jobs were not easy to come by.

To avoid this kind of mass exodus at the end of the year when bonuses are paid, my company adds a 0.5 percent bonus on quarterly targets and a 0.25 percent bonus on reaching the end-of-year target. While this total sum is slightly greater than a 13th-month bonus, it maintains motivation over the entire year. Consequently, our turnover is below the industry standard, at 16 percent.

More Stick, Less Carrot

The "leader is commander" concept has long been discredited by major Western companies, but both the education system and most Chinese companies still operate by it. Consequently, it is often a shock to Western managers who arrive in China to find that the modus operandi still includes more use of the proverbial stick than is common back home. And in my experience, this is still what is needed to accommodate the relative maturity level.

Case in point—throughout 2008, and with the global financial crisis affecting the morale of my entire team, the frequency of checking had dropped below the required 1,000-point minimum. Motivating speeches and encouragement from my national sales manager seemed to have little impact. When he resigned in January 2009, I reassessed his method and took steps to turn things around. I warned the staff that a verbal warning would be given to any salesperson who failed to meet the 1,000-point minimum at the end of February, and should anyone fail again this would be upgraded to a more serious written warning. After two written warnings, the third mistake would be a dismissal. No exceptions—even for the three salespeople who usually had the highest sales, but who happened to be at the bottom of the checking ladder.

The result, as you can guess, was a complete turnaround. In February, only two of the 12 salespeople were under 1,000 points, and only just. By March, the entire team was well clear of the minimum, and sales predictably began to rise. Understandably, so too did the team's morale.

Increase Responsibilities over Time and with Support

Don't be fooled by age. As mentioned earlier, Chinese workers in their 30s tend to have an amount of hands-on experience similar to that of Western employees in their early 20s. Therefore, introduce responsibilities slowly, and be sure to provide support as those responsibilities grow. In particular, be aware that the collectivist culture makes it challenging for newly appointed Chinese managers to supervise their former colleagues. Be sure to enforce the chain of command—otherwise, the manager will be skipped in communication, teamwork will falter, and motivation will follow suit.

And finally, on the topic of motivation, a close friend, who ran a series of gyms under an American franchise in Beijing and northern provinces in China, once highlighted the talent shortage, particularly among the *Balinghou* and the occasional *Jiulinghou* (1990s generation). "I hire for a positive attitude alone, as work experience is a luxury," he said.

THE MEETING

Once your team is motivated and is familiar with the concepts of the target acquisition equation, they can apply them in a real-life situation—the meeting. You've heard the old saying, "You never have a second chance to make a first impression"—that's as true in China as it is in the West.

When Does a Meeting Begin?

Paul, Cecilia, and I walked through the gate of Joy Construction in the Tianjin Economic Development Area, also known as TEDA. Paul was my company's Tianjin sales manager, and Cecelia was his top account manager. As we walked down the service road from the guard post to the front office fifty meters away, a large, heavyset man, over six feet tall, approached. He looked in my direction as we passed, and I instinctively gave him a smile and an Australian "G'day" greeting. He returned the greeting with a South African twang as he continued to walk past.

Within seconds of arriving at the reception desk of the factory, we were ushered into a small meeting room. A minute later John, the purchasing manager, walked in with his HR manager, Amy. We greeted one another using the Chinese custom of exchanging business cards with two hands and then sat down. Moments later a third person walked in. He was the same heavyset man who had passed us earlier on the service road.

"Hi. I'm Derek," he said, as he reached out a large hand to shake. He was our target.

To cut a long story short, we were awarded this training, which happened to be "Negotiation Skills." However, the question to ponder is, "When did this meeting begin?" If you thought "when you shook Derek's hand," you'd be wrong. If it was "when you passed the heavyset man on the road," then you'd be right. I was able to initiate goodwill with that simple "G'day" along the service road, even though I had no idea that I would be seated before the same man.

That story had a happy ending. Now here's one that didn't.

My friend Steven was running late for a sales meeting in Beijing. Under normal circumstances he would have taken the subway. From Dongzhimen to Guomao, where the target was based, would only require one change of the subway line. However, this time he decided to take a taxi. This way, he thought, he could write a few e-mails in the cab. Unfortunately, it seemed that on this day many others had also chosen to forgo the subway. He joined a long line in front of his office waiting for an empty taxi, repeatedly glancing at the hands on his watch as the meeting time drew nearer.

By the time Steven was in a taxi he was frustrated and bad-tempered. And the taxi ride didn't help. The roads were jammed, and the air conditioner was broken. When Steven eventually reached the Guomao building, he had only minutes to spare and he looked a mess. Jumping out of the taxi, he threw some money at the driver, not waiting for the change or receipt, and ran into the building. His tie flapped over his shoulder, and his hair was matted to his face with sweat. Sliding to a halt inside the foyer Steven spied the elevator, and darted in its direction. He tapped the "up" button, as his head turned left and right hoping to see one of the shaft doors open. Unfortunately for Steven, over sixty meters above, a dormant elevator was just coming to life and beginning its slow decent.

Time passed slowly. Steven paced from left to right. What seemed like hours passed, and finally Steven's impatience was broken by the "ding" of the arriving elevator. Even before the door was fully open, Steven was running through, almost knocking over a young woman who was exiting, carrying files.

"Sorry!" he managed to mumble in embarrassment as the woman huffed in disgust.

Turning quickly, Steven's eye's focused on the bank of buttons before him, searching for the button for the nineteenth floor.

"Come on, come on. Where are you?" he said under his breath. "Ah! There you are!"

The 19th-floor button lit up under his finger, and instinctively he reached for the "close" button.

"Come on! Come on!" He had two minutes to spare. Why were the doors taking so long to shut. This was going to be tight! And then a voice shouted from outside the elevator.

"Wait a moment! Hang on!"

Steven looked through the narrowing gap to see a man running toward him.

"Sorry," he thought to himself, and continued jabbing at the "close" button. The doors sealed and Steven was left facing his own flustered reflection. Sweat trickled down his face, the knot of his tie was half open, and the bottom of his shirt protruded over his trousers. However, when the door on the nineteenth floor opened with a "ding," a calm, relaxed and well groomed Steven walked casually from the elevator. He turned right, and walked toward the open door of his prospective target's office. He even had a smile on his face. He had made it in time!

In mid-stride, Steven whipped out a business card from his jacket top pocket and approached the reception desk.

"Hi there," he said with a smile, "I'm here for Mr. Wang. Here's my card, I'm Steven."

"OK, Steven," said the receptionist, "He'll be with you in a moment. He hasn't returned from lunch yet." Steven couldn't believe his luck.

"Please take a seat," she finished.

Steven turned and sat down in the plush couch. He reached for a magazine on the side table and took no notice of a figure as it dashed past him and into the office behind the receptionist. The only sound was the tapping of a keyboard as the receptionist completed an e-mail. Minutes passed.

"Hello, Steven?" came a voice.

Steven turned to face a man; somehow familiar.

"Oh, you're Steven?!" continued the voice—its tone suddenly changed. "I don't have any time for you." The chill was not lost on Steven. "You can leave."

Who was this man? The question of "when does a close begin?" is posed at the beginning of our training sessions.

"When you introduce yourself to the client," say some.

"When you announce your name."

"When you walk into the room."

The responses from trainees, before they hear the story of Steven, vary. What's consistent is that they are all incorrect. By now you've probably figured out that Steven's "Mr. Wang" was also the same man running for the elevator, Mr. "Wait a moment! Hang on!" So when did Steven's sales meeting begin? That's right, in the elevator, not the boardroom. The salesperson does not dictate when a sale begins. A sale begins when the target or KII sees us. For Steven, that was in the elevator, but it could be as you jump out of a taxi, as you get on a train, or as you enter the bathroom. My rule of thumb is to remember that your sales meeting has begun when you leave the privacy of your own home. And that's why I ask myself every time I step out of the car at the client's office, "When does a close begin?" It's a rhetorical question, of course. It just reminds me to be ready at all times. "Lights! Camera! Action!"

As I said, you never know when the check begins. Your target could be watching you from the office window as you leave your taxi or car, or be in the same elevator as you make your way to the meeting. However, assume you make it, unobserved in any unfortunate behavior, to the reception.

The Reception

As you walk through the glass doors, you smile at the receptionist. You're thinking, "Hey, I'm about to impress your manager with a mind-blowing solution." Meanwhile, the receptionist is thinking, "Here comes another sales rep who thinks it's possible to impress the boss with a mind-blowing solution." That's the fact, so drop the arrogance. Instead, look at this first step as an opportunity. You've already read that the receptionist is an alternative source of information. Make small talk, and if possible, funnel the receptionist for information.

If it's cold out, take off your overcoat. When the target or KII eventually arrives, they aren't going to be bundled up, so neither should you. This follows the mirroring concept. Take a seat, and if there's a company brochure or magazine displayed, flick through it. Take notice of any company mission and vision statements that may be displayed in the marketing material, or on the wall. Take particular interest in any reference to values that support your product or service.

The Greeting and Small Talk

The initial meeting with the target is often the most daunting part of the sales process, especially if the target is older, well educated, and from a large company. I lived that challenge for four years when I was in my early 20s and working as a sales representative for Hoechst Marion Roussel, which then merged into Aventis, which proceeded to merge into Sanofi-Aventis. When I first started, I was the youngest representative in the entire company. The prospect of promoting pharmaceutical products to doctors twice my age was more than daunting, it was horrifying. Thankfully, the recruiting officer misread my facial expression as eagerness.

On the first sales call, I imagined I was 16 again, walking into a bottle shop in Metung, Victoria, Australia, to buy a UDL Vodka and Orange six-pack. Shane, my mate, was waiting outside, literally a day older, but lacking the early sprout of facial hair that gave me a chance to convince shopkeepers that I was 18. My heart was racing because, after all, I was attempting to break the law. However, the shame of being turned away would be an even bigger embarrassment. So, acting as if I'd just smoked a pack of cigarettes, walked away from a string of ex-girlfriends, and just finished modifying my Monaro (an Australian iconic car), I walked into the bottle shop. An electronic chime announced my arrival, and I made a silent prayer. Thankfully, either the shopkeeper felt sorry for me or the whole act worked. I retained that act for another nine years as I moved between medical clinic and waiting room, promoting antibiotics and cardiovascular drugs. All in all, acting a little older did me no harm. It also helped that I had a serious case of premature graying, so that by 24 my locks matched my dad's—and he was 56 years old.

Back to you. You find yourself sitting in the target's reception area, as the target approaches from the side door leading to the banks of cubicles beyond. You stand up, placing the company brochure on the side table, smile, and take a few steps forward as the target approaches. As everyone who's done even a little bit of business in China knows it is the business card, or "name card" as it translates directly from Chinese, that is exchanged at the outset of the meeting, and usually before any handshakes. Just as important, the business card is presented with two hands, as if you are handing the target an expensive gift. After this point, though, the four Chinese generations may respond differently.

The *Balinghou* and the Children of the Revolution will generally say their own name as they hand you their business card. They already know who you are and so often say, "Good afternoon, Mr. Jones, my name is Wangwei." Often, particularly if you are Western, these two generations will follow this sentence with a handshake, regardless of your gender or theirs. These two generations are by far the most accommodating with their greetings.

The older Old Red Guards and the True Reds, on the other hand, may simply look down at the card and say, "Ah. Mr. Jones." Often there is no handshake, and if they don't have a business card themselves, you may be left wondering who it is you are talking to. This is even more common with Chinese government officials, who rarely present a card at a meeting. Therefore, prepare in advance and know whom you are going to meet.

Seating Arrangements

Next, the target asks you to follow them to the meeting room. In China, it is tradition for the host to sit facing the door. This is a sign of respect, and originates from feng shui beliefs suggesting a sign of power—and of reduced danger of being attacked from behind. If you walk in with a Chinese target, then take the seat with your back to the door. Or even better, ask the target where he would like you to sit. If you are led to the meeting room by the receptionist or the target's assistant, then play it safe and sit with your back to the door. In this day and age you have little chance of being attacked by assassins, so give your target the illusion of strength.

That doesn't mean that seating arrangements are not important. Quite the contrary. While the sales call might start with you and the target sitting opposite each other, that's not how you want to spend most of your meeting. Facing one another creates a sense of "us and them" just as in a game of soccer, rugby, or American football. Don't worry so much about where you and the target sit with respect to the door, rather, focus on how easily you could skirt around during the meeting to sit beside the target. Sitting beside your target, shoulder-to-shoulder rather than across a table, instantly creates camaraderie. If you happen to be in the meeting with a colleague, then your colleague should remain opposite the target or KII, because when they speak you will be nodding in agreement with them. As you are seated on the side of the target or KII you will be sending unconscious messages that the target's side of the table agrees with what your colleague is saying. Essentially you become a KII.

Avoiding Storybooking

Once you are seated, it is likely that the target or KII will say, "Tell me about your business." Avoid the urge to broadcast your company's past successes and key advantages over competitors. Come lunchtime, your target isn't going to remember any of your propaganda, so instead turn the question 180 degrees.

Say something like this: "Sure. I could tell you all about our company. After all, we've been in business for 26 years and work with most of the Fortune 500. However, rather than bore you with details that might not be relevant, do you mind if I ask you a few questions?

Or perhaps: "Before I introduce our business, do you mind if I ask you a few questions? That way I can save you time and introduce only what's important to your needs."

Chances are the target will say "sure!" Most people like to hear themselves talk, so use that psychological phenomenon to your advantage. And by turning the question on its head, you give yourself the opportunity to find the target's needs. The alternative is to *storybook* the target, and that will just bore them.

Case in point: I once sat in my own boardroom, listening to the worst sales pitch ever. Moments after introducing himself, Graham had flipped open his laptop, connected the digital projector, and was flipping page after page through his presentation, reading the words on the slide as if I was blind—a classic case of storybooking. By slide five I was almost in a coma, so I asked him a question.

"I'll get to that in a moment," he replied. That "moment" was 23 slides later. Not only did I not buy his product (an online language program), I almost threw him out of my office. Luckily for him, I was too lethargic.

Most salespeople don't listen. They equate the title of "salesperson" with "talker," and they think that the target seated before them is as interested in their product or service as they are. Unfortunately, they are wrong. The target cares little about what you have to offer. All they need is a benefit—a solution to their problem—and uncovering their need is the first step in building desire.

As a result, most salespeople storybook their product or service in the first few minutes of meeting the client. Just like reading a bedtime story to a child, the salesperson starts at page one and flips through each page of the sales brochure or PowerPoint file—page one, page two, page three, ... Not surprisingly, both the child and the target end up asleep by the end.

The key to a great sales call is to funnel. Funneling involves a questioning strategy that begins with open questions. An open question could be "How's business?" or "What has your department been doing recently?" or "What kind of problems are you facing at the moment?" These open, non-leading questions ensure that you do not assume you know what problems your target is facing.

And funneling doesn't have to begin with your target. It can begin much earlier, with your alternative sources of information—the receptionist and the engineers.

Funneling

I'll go out on a limb and say that most salespeople never funnel. They get the gist of the technique, and they might even have tried it a few times, but they fall back into old habits—to pitch their target with their own opinion as to why their product or service is the best and how it beats all competition. A pitch is just like a pickup line. Everyone has one, but few have success using it. And yet, like pickup lines, sales pitches prevail even though those who use them are ultimately *losers*. The solution is to *funnel*, that is, to use structured questioning.

A funnel, as you know, has a large opening at the top, then it gradually gets smaller and eventually turns into a tube. People use funnels in the garage to poor oil into engines, and in the kitchen to decant liquids from large containers into small ones. The conical shape makes it easy to pour into the right general area, while the output tube directs the liquid into the exact spot you want. The funnel questioning technique works just the same way. The questions you use at first are broader, and as the conversation continues, you narrow your questions down. Being general at first keeps you from making assumptions that could lead you down the wrong path. Here's an example:

"Hi. Thanks for seeing me today," you say to your target.

"That's fine, so tell me about your business," says the target.

"Perhaps I could get a better understanding of your business, so I can save you time, instead. Do you mind if I ask you some questions first?" you counter.

"OK. That makes sense. Go on."

(This is where you begin to funnel . . . .)

"So, I'm interested to know what kind of sales training your company has done in the past."

Fail! You've just funneled too quickly, that is, you were too specific, too early in the conversation. Instead of asking what sales training your target has undertaken in the past, you should be less specific and ask, "So, I'm interested to know what kind of training your company has done in the past."

In the first question, where you asked the target about "sales training," the answer could have been, "No. We've never done sales training before," and consequently you might incorrectly assume that that means that your target has not done *any* training before. However, when you are more open and ask about "training" in general, the target is likely to give a more useful answer.

"So, I'm interested to know what kind of training your company has done in the past," you ask, omitting the word "sales" ahead of "training."

"We schedule all of our salespeople to do presentation training each year. Some also do time management training," the target replies. Bingo!

You would have missed the point about time management completely if you'd only asked about sales training. That's why the first set of questions are defined as non-leading and open (see Figure 9.1). By *non-leading* I mean that you are not putting words into your target's mouth. *Open* means that a responsive answer has to be more than yes or no. So, "What are you looking for in a vacuum cleaner?" is a non-leading, open question, whereas "Do you want your vacuum cleaner to be lightweight?" is a leading, closed question. Until you raised the issue of weight your target might never have considered weight as important, but now that you mention it, the target is likely to say something like, "Sure, who wants a heavy vacuum cleaner." When you ask leading, closed questions you hear about the need that you expect, which is not necessarily a need that the target regards as important.

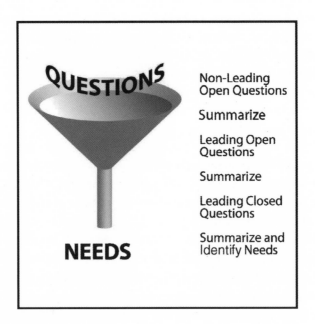

FIGURE 9.1 The Funnel Technique

Once your target starts to list possible needs you can then start to shape the discussion by using leading, open questions. These types of questions are ideal to clarify statements that may be ambiguous:

- ■ "So when you say you want reliability in a vacuum cleaner, what do you mean?"
- ■ "I understand that you want a vacuum that is great value for money. Please tell me more about your definition of value."

Remember, open questions don't have to start with *how, what, when, where, who,* or *why*. They can also employ "tell me more," "I'd like to hear more about," or simply "Go on." As long as the target has to provide more information to answer you and not reply with a yes or no, then you have asked an open question.

At times you are going to run out of things to say. This is a perfect time to summarize what your target has said, while showing that you paid attention.

"Just so I know that I fully understood you, I'd like to summarize what you just said. You said . . . "

This technique is also a great way to build goodwill. Each time you repeat what the target has already said, then they are going to agree, and each time they do this, they are reinforcing a positive habit with you and your company. William Ury refers to this as "accumulating yeses," and it's directly linked to the positive language that I have already discussed in Chapter 5, in the context of goodwill.

Matching Features to Needs

Harold S. Geneen once said, "Facts from paper are not the same as facts from people. The reliability of the people giving you the facts is as important as the facts themselves." He was the CEO of ITT in the United States, and turned it from a firm with US$760 million sales in 1961 into a multinational conglomerate with US$17 billion in sales in 1970. No doubt he had to persuade a number of people for that rapid growth, and he would have done this by matching his company's features with his targets' needs. So how do you verbalize this match?

Say that you uncover that your target's need is geographical scope of the service in question. The target's firm has factories in multiple cities, and you also have staff in each of those cities. You believe you have matched this need, so you say:

"Okay. So from our conversation it seems that you have a number of locations where services like ours are required, and therefore I'd like to show you the locations of our current offices, which, you'll be happy to see, match closely with your locations."

Alternatively, your funneling may reveal that the target is risk averse, and so you say:

"From what you've said, it sounds as if you have had a rough time with some of your suppliers in the past. I can understand your being wary of untested suppliers, and so I'd like to give you this list showing you our Fortune 500 clients with their testimonials. There is also a phone number after each name that you can call to confirm their satisfaction levels."

If you are in procurement and dealing with a supplier, you might say something like this:

"I understand that you are having a tough time during this global financial crisis, and that cash flow is tight. It just so happens that I am authorized to permit up-front payment of suppliers, should an attractive discount be offered."

Don't assume that your target can guess that you have a match. Spell it out clearly, and highlight the benefits of the match.

And that means using evidence, that is, your features folder. A hint for all sales managers, though—make sure your sales team brings the complete features folder. It might seem like common sense to bring everything—after all, how can anyone possibly predict all the questions a target is going to ask? Unfortunately, in my 10 years of experience this assumption is wrong; salespeople almost always do assume they can predict what they'll need. When you leave the office check your staff's equipment, and don't leave it up to chance.

Involving Your Target

A great way to rapidly build goodwill with your target, using the theory of reciprocation, is to involve your target in the sales process. During the meeting, I will ask the target or KII, "May I give you a quick demonstration? It will only take five minutes, and you'll be able to use this technique after this meeting." To date, none of my targets have ever declined to improve themselves, particularly if it only takes five minutes. Actually, it normally takes two or three times that, but by the five-minute mark the target or KII is so engrossed that it doesn't matter.

Another technique is to ask for assistance during the meeting. This could be in setting up the projector, turning off the lights, or acting in an activity. Engaging the target during the sales meeting creates an unconscious ownership of your cause and hence builds buy-in when the time comes to sign the contract.

The Wrap-Up

Before leaving the meeting you must inform the target or KII of the next step. Usually that is providing a proposal, either in written or digital form. Ask the target when the proposal should arrive—and then be very sure to get it there by that time, or sooner. As discussed later in the chapter, your target's satisfaction depends heavily on how well you meet expectations.

RECORDING INFORMATION

Throughout the entire sales call you should be recording your discussion with the target in a systematic process. This is because any CRM system is only as good as the information that it receives. Moving information from the meeting into the database allows for errors, so it is important to have a structured way of recording the information gleaned from funneling.

My team and I developed what we call a "sales companion," which is half-page-sized ring binder that keeps the meeting check information neatly together. We have the book produced en masse for about US$3.50 (23 CNY) each. With a program such as Microsoft Publisher or Adobe InDesign you could quite easily produce something along these lines and print it on your company's photocopier.

I'll describe each of the sections in detail, so you understand how each field is to be used.

Pre-Meeting Page

As the name suggests, the pre-meeting page should be completed before the meeting. If you are a sales manager who accompanies your team to meetings, then you can look at this page and instantly know that your subordinate is fully prepared. Remember, "If you can't measure, you can't manage." "I know all about the company" is not as measurable as looking down the page and seeing each field in the sales companion completed.

■ *Date and Time:* These fields allow you to archive your completed sales companion forms and review them if you ever need to correct data you have entered into your CRM system.

■ *Contact Name:* This is the name or names of the target or KII that you are going to meet. Again, this is valuable information to archive for future reference.

■ *Contact Info:* You are traveling to the target's office when you suddenly realize you don't have their address, and you can't call them because you don't have their number. It's all on the company CRM system, back in the office. This is the purpose of this field—to get you out of trouble.

■ *Company Name:* Obviously this is useful for archiving your information. For a sales manager, this line is also useful to test the staff's pronunciation of the target's company name. My company's national sales manager, Mike, escorted his subordinate, David, to a meeting with flavors and fragrances giant, Givaudan. This name is hard enough to spell, let alone pronounce, and David was clearly poor at both, calling the company "Giv-all-dem" (very far from correct, which would sound more like "Jiv-or-dun") and forgetting how to spell its name. When Mike asked for a briefing before heading off to the meeting he quickly realized that David needed some training to avoid embarrassment in front of the target.

■ *Competitors:* Many salespeople underestimate the power of name dropping. If you happen to have worked with the target's competitor in the past, then this is an excellent feature. Why do women find men with girlfriends more attractive? For the same reasons your target will find your business more attractive for working with their competitor—preselection. If a competitor has used your services, or in the case of dating, believes you suitable as a partner, then this makes you more valuable in the eyes of others.

I use Hoovers (www.hoovers.com) to research competitors. It includes a "Competitors List" for most large listed companies, particularly those from the United States. It's then easy for me to run a search on each of my target's competitors on my own CRM to see if we have trained them previously. Even in the case that we haven't trained them, we have often contacted their HR department and may know key members of the staff. Again, this gives you names to drop.

■ *Country Headquarters:* You'd never walk into a job interview naive about that company. Therefore, you should never be naive about a company you are trying to sell to. The "country headquarters" field may not be so important when doing business in the United States, as most of the targets' company HQs are probably based there. However, in China your target's HQ is as likely to be in Chicago as in Berlin or Melbourne. Again, use Hoovers to get the details before you head off to the meeting.

■ *Past Sales:* As I mentioned under the "Competitors" field, you will become more attractive as a vendor if you are preselected. Your company will become even more attractive if you have done business with the target's company in the past. You might think that the target already knows that, but don't assume this. In our CRM system, Philips in China includes Philips & Lighting Luminaire, Philips & Yaming Lamp, Philips Shenzhen, Philips Tianjin, Philips China Investment, Philips DAP, Philips Design, Philips Display System, Philips Domestic Household Appliance . . . I'll stop now. We have another 11 separate Philips entities in our database, and each has a separate target. We hadn't trained all of these entities, but we had trained at least four, and on a visit to one of the entities that we had yet to train, we'd be silly not to mention our preselection, wouldn't we?

■ *Language of Meeting:* Again, this is not going to be a problem if your meetings are in Australia, Britain, or the United States, but in China and Europe there is a chance that English may not be the language of choice during the meeting. Be prepared. If you know this in advance, you can bring a translator, or brush up on your Spanish, Mandarin, or Esperanto.

■ *Language Ability:* If you are unable to speak the target or KII's native language and don't have a translator, then you may have to conduct the meeting at a slower pace, particularly if your contact's English ability is poor. This field will just prepare you.

■ *Other Important Info:* This is where you mention that the target's face has a birthmark, or that your wife happens to know the target's wife—important information to ignore or bring up, respectively.

Debrief Page

Debriefing is as important as pre-meeting preparation. This informa-tion will let you prepare a more customized proposal, one that meets all of the target's needs.

■ *Reflective:* This is where you record the idiomatic language used by the target. For example, at a meeting in 2008 with alcohol giant Diageo, one of the targets said that she would like to "marry" two training programs together. She didn't say *join* or *connect;* she said *marry.* She is probably unaware that she uses this term, but I knew that on an unconscious level she would relate to this personal expres-sion when it appeared in my proposal.

■ *Needs:* In this space you define what needs you believe the target has. Is the main need for speed, reliability, scope, or expertise, for example? Ensure that this need becomes the focus of your proposal.

■ *Features:* If you have been able to uncover the target's needs, then which features does your company have that can match them? If the target indicated that scope of service is an issue, then, in your proposal, you should mention that you have offices in each of the target's cities.

■ *Next Check:* As noted earlier, it took my firm 87 checks with Maersk Shipping to get our first contract. And there have been many more checks since that first signing. Just because you have had a meet-ing and funneled the targets for their need, that doesn't mean that they won't use your competitor. You have to keep your name in the forefront of your target's mind. What will your next check be? A thank-you e-mail the following day? The proposal on the upcoming Thursday? Or sending tickets to next week's industry conference?

■ *Deadline:* Don't ruin your goodwill by missing your promised deadline. That deadline could be related to sending a proposal or simply calling back to arrange a meeting. This is all associated with what I call the "satisfaction equation." Minding this equation will ensure that you keep your target or KII happy when you make promises. It is created by dividing the perceived value for the target by the target's expectations.

$$\text{Satisfaction} = \text{Perceived Value}/\text{Expectation}$$

When you tell targets that you will give them the proposal on Thursday, then they will expect that proposal by Thursday. Therefore their *Expectation* is always equal to 100 percent. If you promise to deliver on Thursday, and *do* deliver on that day, then your satisfaction equation is 100 percent divided by 100 percent, which equals one. A satisfaction equation result of one means "good enough," but that's all.

However, if you tell your target that you will deliver the proposal on Thursday, but you are late, the perceived value of your service is reduced, possibly by half. Consequently your satisfaction equation result is 50 percent divided by 100 percent, which equals one-half. Any score below one is equal to "not good enough."

Likewise, when you promise to deliver the proposal on Thursday, and deliver two days earlier, you increase the perceived value, maybe as much as 200 percent. When you divide 200 percent by 100 percent, your result is a number greater than one; two to be exact. That is the goal of sales. Always create satisfaction greater than one, because a score of one is only good enough, it's not great. Ensure that you are fully aware of your target's expectations, and you meet that deadline with a smile.

■ *Additional Note:* In my company's sales companion we include Hewitt-Gleeson's *GBB* concept (1990). *GBB* stands for "Good, Bad,

Better," and is a reminder that all sales calls can be improved. What was good about the check? What was bad? And, more important, how could we improve next time, to make it better? Sales managers should use GBB after every sales meeting in which they escorted a subordinate. Noting down what the subordinate did that was good or bad, and how they can make it better next time, will increase the speed of on-the-job learning.

The next pages in the sales companion are blank and are dedicated to recording the comments of the target or KII. Again this needs to be done in a structured manner so no information is left out for the CRM system.

Another habit of mine is writing the names of the meeting attendees on the top right-hand corner of my sales companion. And here's why. In China, as in Japan, it is the norm for all parties to present their business cards to one another at the beginning of the meeting. A salesperson who is meeting, say, three people will collect three business cards before even sitting down, and will set out the cards on the table to serve as a quick reference for the participants' names. Disaster is moments away, however. That same salesperson, eager to show some features, carelessly flops a company brochure on the table, covering the three carefully aligned business cards. As is so often the case, the salesperson gets caught up in the excitement of talking, instead of asking questions, and then realizes that the business cards have disappeared under a pile of reports and statistics. And the cards are stuck down there, as fishing them out would damage goodwill by revealing that the names have been forgotten.

Therefore, follow my lead and write the names of the participants on the top of your notebook. If you are right-handed then you should write these names in the upper right corner of the page, in the order their owners are sitting. If you are left-handed, then you should write the names in the upper left. If you use these specific locations, then you need only look over your pen as you continue to write to refresh your memory for the names. This act will be unnoticeable. The targets or KIIs will have no idea that you are forgetful, and so you don't lose goodwill.

Once you have recorded the participants' names, the next step is to record their pet phrases so you can use reflective language, both in the meeting and in the final proposal. In the previous example of reflective language with Diageo, I wrote the phrase, "like to marry the two training programs together" in quotation marks in my notebook. The quotation marks indicate that that was exactly what the target said. I even underlined the word "marry," to remind myself to use that specific term when I summarized the target's thoughts while funneling and writing the proposal.

THE PROPOSAL

I am often shocked by the poor quality of proposals that originate from Chinese sales teams. Regardless of whether it is a proposal for a conference at a hotel or for the purchase of raw materials for a mining conglomerate there is clearly a weakness regarding quality control.

Tim, a procurement manager for a large mining company with offices in Shanghai, concurs. As a native English speaker, he finds himself being asked to double-check proposals that are full of obvious nonstandard formatting, incorrect fonts, and outdated information and images. Tim says this lack of an eye for detail is extremely frustrating, because his Chinese staff almost expect him to finish their work for them, and over the four years that he has been in China he has seen that this problem is common across many organizations.

Again, the cause of this problem can be traced back to the Chinese education system, which is focused on rote learning. Students are not taught to solve problems but rather to follow the rules set by teachers. From my personal experience in the field of corporate training, trainees ask for packaged templates to cover all problems, rather than taking the concept and learning to apply it to multiple scenarios. Consequently, when you ask your sales team to "produce an attractive proposal based on the client's needs," the result is understandably varied.

However, once you are aware of this cultural phenomenon, problems with proposal quality can be solved simply by adding standards. While it is very time-consuming, in the long run creating well-documented standards regarding proposals will help ensure quality. And while posting examples on a bulletin board might seem somewhat childish, remember that you are working with a relatively immature team—people who, even if they are in their 30s, have less than 10 years of sales experience.

Part Three

The Negotiation

CHAPTER **10**

Negotiating with Your Target

When a man says that he approves of something in principle, it means he hasn't the slightest intention of carrying it out in practice.
—Otto von Bismarck (1815–1898)

Once you've applied the ideas discussed thus far, you are 90 percent of the way. The target has agreed in principle with your offer, you've met a number of KIIs, and a date has been set for delivery. Time to count your chickens, right? I wish it was that simple. Even with a contract signed by both parties, the whole relationship could go pear-shaped before you see a cent, penny, or fen. No chicken counting until the money's in the bank. You are still in the danger zone. As Otto von Bismarck suggests, at any point now, the target could make unreasonable demands. These demands could be linked to price, volume, delivery, maintenance, or any number of odd requests. However, what they want and what you give them both depend on one thing—leverage. So what is it?

LEVERAGE

Leverage is the negotiating term for power. However, that doesn't mean it has anything to do with strength. There are countless

David-and-Goliath tales where the logically stronger party was beaten by the lesser party. Here are few examples:

Michael Dell versus IBM

At age 19 and armed with only US$1000, Michael Dell abandoned plans to become a doctor, dropped out of college, and told his father he was going to compete against IBM. This was in the pre-Internet days, and "Big Blue" was the big dog in town. By the time Dell was 22 years old, his company had achieved annual sales of about US$150 million; it is now a US$57 billion company. It maintains the leading market share in the United States.

Robert (Bob) Kearns versus Ford and Chrysler

Kearns filed a lawsuit against Ford Motor Company in 1978 and Chrysler Corporation in 1982 for patent infringement of his intermittent windscreen wiper design. Both cases were later heard in the 1990s. Ford lost and agreed to settle with Kearns for US$10.2 million. Chrysler was ordered to pay US$18.7 million with interest, equaling approximately US$30 million.

Democratic Republic of Vietnam (North Vietnam) versus the United States

The Vietnam War (1959–1975) took the lives of between 3 and 4 million Vietnamese, but comparatively fewer American lives at 58,159. Furthermore, many of the offensives launched by the North Vietnamese, such as Tet, were huge tactical failures. Nevertheless, Ho Chi Minh and his government were confident that they would win the war. They knew their opponent's weakness: public opinion, which was quickly turning against the U.S. government. Aerial bombing of North Vietnam had halted, and the United States had opened up negotiations on how to end the war. The North Vietnamese simply delayed negotiations, including a debate over the shape of the conference table. Today, it's easy to recognize these tactics from the teachings of Roger Fisher and William Ury. In *Getting to Yes*, they point out, "The more easily and happily you can walk away from a negotiation, the greater your capacity to affect its outcome."

This last example highlights the ultimate irony of negotiations. Power, or leverage, is not what you have but what you are willing to lose. This is true power. Michael Dell was a university student funded by his parents. What did he have to lose, compared to "Big Blue"? Robert Kearns was financially stable and wasn't desperate for a multi-million-dollar payout. And finally, the North Vietnamese were willing to lose 50 of their own for one American life. Current news reports from Afghanistan and Iraq prove that the U.S. government has yet to learn from its earlier military disasters.

Now to better describe leverage in a business environment, again I have to borrow from Fisher and Ury (1983) to discuss its two parts: neediness and BATNA (see Figure 10.1).

Neediness

Dale Carnegie (1888–1955) said, "When dealing with people, remember you are not dealing with creatures of logic, but creatures of emotion." We've all been needy at one time or another, whether as children requiring our parents' attention, adolescents with a crush on a high school classmate, or at any age and spotting the jacket that we just had to have. While we like to think we make decisions rationally,

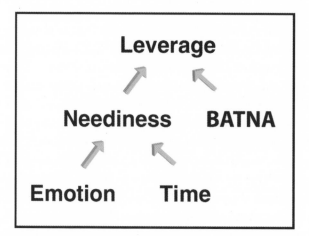

FIGURE 10.1 Leverage and Its Parts

there's a great deal of truth in Dale Carnegie's statement that we are all "creatures of emotion."

Auctions of apartments and houses take advantage of this fact. They allow potential buyers to envision their lives in the new abode and then quickly bombard this emotion with the addition of competition and a finite deadline. The auctioneers use potential buyers' neediness against them. I simplify this process into the following equation:

$$\text{Neediness} = \text{Increasing Emotion} + \text{Reducing Time}$$

Falling in love with anyone, or anything for that matter, increases emotion. When a deadline is introduced, that is, reducing time, it eats away at the period in which to negotiate for the desired person or object, and this in turn increases neediness further. Therefore, your goal in a negotiation is to reduce the effect of both, or at any rate to convince your target that you have done so. In negotiating, perception is reality. Here's an example:

In October 2008 I was in a bit of a dilemma. I had arrived in Beijing without a suit. As I had flown on a weekend, I had dressed casually for the flight and forgotten to pack formal wear for meetings. The following day, Monday, I got up early to see if the local shopping center had a reasonably cheap suit in my size. Strangely, there was only one suit shop in the entire complex, and the only suit that didn't make me look like a middle-aged science teacher was a size too small. Worried, I called my colleagues, who relieved my stress.

"There's a silk market opposite the training venue. Go there."

Thirty minutes later, I was standing before a four-story building with only 45 minutes before I was to introduce the keynote speaker. My need was clear—speed. And my neediness was high.

I twisted through the tourist-filled aisles, made more difficult by the wheelchair-riding Canadian Para Olympic team who just happened to be there, shopping for fake Louis Vuitton and North Face.

Several of the three-by-three-meter stalls stocked suits. Most of these suits bordered on tacky, but a tan, "Englishman-in-Singapore sipping gin and tonics-esque" number caught my attention. It had

a faint pinstripe and would go with the white shirt that I was currently wearing with my jeans. The only issue was that I had 25
minutes to negotiate, buy, dress, and cross the six-lane road to the
business center. While my need for speed was clear, it was still
only known to me.

Had the salesgirl asked me how my day was, what I was up to, or
for what occasion I would wear my suit, she might have been able to
discover my desperation. With that knowledge, she could simply delay
my progress—having me try on the trousers in her stall, playing with
the length, and chattering about how good I looked in the suit. Had
she done that, my neediness would have increased with every rotation
of the minute hand, and she could have increased the price of the suit.
But she didn't. Instead, she fell back on habit, and the following conversation resulted:

"How much you want to pay?" she asked, in almost perfect
English.

"That's a good question. There are lots of suits in this place. How
much do you want to sell it for?" I replied.

I already knew the rough price, and (assuming that she'd fall into
the positional sales trap) I had a price ready that would mean that our
halfway meeting point would be what I wanted.

"Twelve hundred, OK?! This is good suit."

"Three hundred. There are many suits like this."

"Aiya! So low! One thousand! My lowest price. OK?"

I began to look at the inside of the jacket, pretending I knew something about stitching.

"Hmmm. This isn't so good. I'll give you four hundred. OK? And
I'll buy it now."

"You are killing me. This is a good suit. Best in Beijing!"

"So?"

"OK. Nine hundred. My final price!" she wasn't doing anything to
suppress her emotion.

"Five hundred. I'll pay you now."

"No! Six hundred. Come on!"

"Four-fifty and done." My watch showed I had about 15 minutes left.

"Five hundred, OK?!"

"OK," I said. I wanted to make her feel like she won something, even though I had just dropped her price by almost two-thirds, and paid less than $US80 for a suit.

As soon as money and suit had changed hands, my poker face cracked, and I frantically made my way to the tailor at the back of the building to get the leg length adjusted. I had 10 minutes before I had to introduce a guest speaker, but thankfully the tailor was like Michael Schumacher on the sewing machine. With two minutes to spare, I found myself freshly dressed and standing in front of the audience. No one knew that I had just negotiated for the clothing that I was standing in. For the record, I've since worn that suit more than you'd assume its price tag would allow.

So, what's the moral of the story? If the salesgirl had funneled me and found my need, which was speed, she could have controlled my neediness and thus lowered my leverage. Instead, she fell back on the habit of positional negotiation. And that habit cost her; literally.

BATNA

Understanding your "best alternative to a negotiated agreement," or BATNA, is part of "Negotiating 101." It's a scary-sounding acronym, but all it is is a way of saying "Plan B"—or "Plan C, D, E, and F," for that matter. If you don't get what you want and have to walk away from this negotiation, what will you do? If Plan B is just as attractive to you as a negotiated solution, then you have a strong BATNA. If Plans C, D, and E are equally good, then you are laughing. Alternatively, if your options are much less attractive, or worse, nonexistent, then you are said to have a weak BATNA.

Back in 2005 I watched a negotiating battle unfold before my eyes. Thankfully I was not involved, so I was able to watch from the sidelines, while taking notes for this book. One of the parties was the British Council, a non-governmental organization based in the United Kingdom, which specializes in international educational and cultural opportunities.

A major function of the British Council is to arrange and co-ordinate International English Language Testing System (IELTS) examinations for Chinese who wish to study or emigrate to Australia,

Canada, New Zealand, or, of course, the United Kingdom. The examination is carried out by native-English-speaking teachers, who must first complete their own certificate—an English teaching certificate, often referred to as a TEFL (for Teaching English as a Foreign Language)—before undertaking the British Council qualification. Only then can someone be considered as an examiner for IELTS examinations.

The problem started when a new clause was introduced into the IELTS examiner contract. This clause stated that the IELTS examiner, not the British Council, would now be responsible for payment of all taxes incurred from employment. The British Council decided to have all IELTS examiners, nationwide, sign the new clause—or else!

"I hadn't marked papers for a while, and actually found out about the new clause from a couple of examiners when I dropped into the British Council offices," said a former IELTS examiner. "There was no formal announcement, and I certainly never received a letter or e-mail, or anything."

Many of the examiners were concerned by the clause, and rumor had it that the new clause potentially opened examiners up for being fined or even jailed for not paying their own personal taxes. True or not, staff were scared. Much of the concern stemmed from a lack of information that had been filled by rumor and a new distrust of the British Council, which seemed to be "passing the buck." But then again, the status quo seemed like the safe option. After all, many examiners reasoned, what would happen if they, as a group, ignored the order to sign the new contract?

And, in fact, the status quo did remain.

"Had it come alongside an increase in pay, then I'm sure a lot of examiners would have signed. But no incentive was offered!"

Consequently, the rollout of the new clause was a failure, as only a small number of examiners signed it. Instead, due to a lack of negotiation and communication with the IELTS examiners, the British Council seemed draconian, and then, when the system failed, it looked weak. The need of the examiner to sign the clause was low. The status quo had been in place for many years, and furthermore there was no benefit related to the signing of the document. The need of the British

Council to have the contract signed was medium to high, as it was a way of reducing tax and risk.

The BATNA of the examiner was overpowering, as there was no consequence in not signing the new contract (losing one's job). However, the BATNA of the British Council, if the examiner did not sign the clause, would be to recruit and hire hundreds of new examiners, which would be very time-consuming and costly. It was therefore no surprise that the IELTS examiners to this day do not pay their income tax.

MEASURING YOUR LEVERAGE

You should measure your leverage prior to going into a negotiation. That way you can choose your battles and decide how tough or soft you will negotiate. Four parts will determine your overall leverage score:

- Your neediness
- Your target's neediness
- Your BATNA
- Your target's BATNA

The final score is from −10 to +10. Any score under zero is a sign of weakness, that is, your target holds more power than you do, and therefore you are unlikely to get what's best for you. That could be either a low or high price, depending on which side of the negotiation table you sit. Accordingly, any score over zero is in your favor. Obviously the closer you are to +10 then the stronger your leverage.

The chart in Figure 10.2 rates neediness.

Remember from Figure 10.1, neediness is a combination of increasing *emotion* and reducing *time*. Think of each in turn. Do you really, really, *really* need this negotiation to succeed? That's not good. Your high emotion makes you weaker in negotiations. Give yourself a score of -1. Now, how are you with time? Do you have plenty of time before you have to sign the contract, or is time running out? And is this limitation on time causing you trouble? If you find yourself biting

	Your Rating
Your Rating	Very High = −2 High = −1 Medium = 0 Low= +1 Very Low = +2	(From −2 to +2)
		Target's Rating
Target's Rating	Very High = +2 High = +1 Medium = 0 Low= −1 Very Low = −2	(From −2 to +2)
Your Total Neediness Rating = Your Rating + Target's Rating		(From −4 to +4)

Weakest −4 −3 −2 −1 0 +1 +2 +3 +4 Strongest

FIGURE 10.2 Neediness Rating

your nails and looking up at the clock every few minutes, then give yourself another −1. Bad news. Your total rating for neediness is −2, or "Very High."

The next task is to uncover the "Target's Rating" for neediness. It's difficult to know what your target is thinking, but if you have used your alternative sources of information and have funneled in depth, then you should have the gist of it. How emotional does your target seem while talking to you? Ranting and arm-waving? Or sitting quietly? If it's the latter, that indicates a low level of emotion. Again, that's not good for you, as it shows a lack of emotional attachment to the success of this negotiation, so give yourself −1. Now, is time a problem for the target as well? Or not as important? If the people on the other side are also looking at the clock and biting their nails, then that's good for you. That means their time pressure is high. That's a score of +1. So for the target's total rating on neediness, you have −1 for emotion and +1 for time, which equals 0.

Now to calculate your total neediness rating, add your neediness of −2 to the target's neediness rating of 0. That makes the value for your total neediness rating equal −2. Life could be better; you're in a weak position. Of course, the above example is completely hypothetical. The result could turn out hundreds of other ways.

The next step is to find out your BATNA Rating, which depends on the quality and number of other choices available to you (see Figure 10.3). The more alternatives, the better.

If you walk away and don't sign the contract with your target, what will happen? Can you walk into the office of another target and sell the same product or service? If you are a buyer, could you buy the same quality product at a similar price from another supplier?

How many alternative buyers or suppliers do you have today? Not tomorrow, today. Right now. If you have some strong alternatives, then that's great (see Figure 10.3). Give yourself a +3 rating.

		Your Rating
Your Rating	Great = +3 Very Good = +2 Good = +1 OK = 0 Bad = -1 Very Bad = -2 Terrible = -3	(From −3 to +3)
		Target's Rating
Target's Rating	Great = -3 Very Good = -2 Good = -1 OK = 0 Bad = +1 Very Bad = +2 Terrible = +3	(From -3 to +3)
Your Total BATNA Rating = Your Rating + Target's Rating		(From −6 to +6)

Weakest −6 −5 −4 −3 −2 −1 0 +1 +2 +3 +4 +5 +6 Strongest

FIGURE 10.3 BATNA Rating

Weakest −10 −9 −8 −7 −6 −5 −4 −3 −2 −1 0 +1 +2 +3 +4 +5 +6 +7 +8 +9 +10 Strongest

FIGURE 10.4 Your Total Leverage Rating (Neediness Plus BATNA)

This is an estimate, a not scientific measurement, so go with your gut feeling.

Now, what about the target's BATNA? Are you the only game in town, or are there alternatives? If so, how many? This is where the more information you have on your target the better. For argument's sake, say that the target's BATNA is bad. There's one alternative, but it's weak. The worse the target's BATNA, the better that is for you, so you can assign a BATNA score of +1. Therefore, your total BATNA rating is +3 plus +1, which equals +4.

To find your total leverage, combine the number from your total neediness rating (Figure 10.2) with the one from your total BATNA rating (Figure 10.3). Your neediness was −2, but your BATNA was +4, giving you a score of +2. As mentioned before, and as shown in Figure 10.4, your possible rating is from −10 to +10. The lower the score, the worse your leverage. The higher the better. So what happens if you're on the wrong side of zero? How do you increase your leverage?

INCREASING YOUR LEVERAGE

You have four ways to increase your leverage:

- Decrease your neediness.
- Increase your target's neediness.
- Increase your BATNA.
- Decrease your target's BATNA.

It is definitely easier to affect your own neediness and BATNA than those of your target. But difficult doesn't mean impossible.

For example, consider the British Council. As noted earlier, this quasi-governmental organization is responsible for helping Chinese students go and study in the United Kingdom. To support this mission, the British Council organizes an information session once a year. At this event, speakers provide information on housing, education, and government resources, and they offer a Q&A session where attendees can ask questions. Between 300 and 500 attendees generally attend. This large number of targets provides an opportunity to cross-sell other companies' services. One of these services is airline flights, and at the time of the negotiation I have in mind, Virgin Atlantic, China Airlines, and China Eastern Airlines provided direct flights from Beijing or Shanghai to London Heathrow. Alternative airlines included Lufthansa, Air France, and Scandinavian Airlines, but these airlines had to stop in their respective countries before flying to London.

In 2006 Virgin Atlantic sponsored the information session and was satisfied with its return on investment (ROI). In 2007, however, the British Council doubled the fee to US$8,000. The British Council regarded this price increase as fair, because at that time return flights to London were at least US$800 before tax. Virgin Atlantic needed to sell only 10 return tickets to break even, and as the event was expected to attract more than 300 attendees, it was highly probable that Virgin Atlantic would see a positive ROI. Of course, there was no guarantee, as attendees could choose airlines for themselves, or not travel to the United Kingdom at all.

I use this case study to introduce the concept of leverage. In my training sessions, I ask my trainees to work in groups to answer seven questions about it. While the questions listed here are aimed at eliciting answers related to the British Council case study, they address the same seven points that you should ask yourself when you begin negotiations with any target:

- Assuming you are the British Council, what concerns might Virgin Atlantic raise at your meeting?
- What kind of information is currently unknown to you?
- Who has stronger leverage? (Calculate it—don't guess!)
- How can you reduce the leverage of Virgin Atlantic?
- How can Virgin Atlantic reduce your leverage?

- What additional benefits could you include that have little value to the British Council but greater value to Virgin Atlantic?
- Who are the stakeholders in this negotiation?

By applying these seven questions to your next negotiation you will start to think like the target and therefore have a better chance of determining your overall leverage. Oh, and by the way, my answers to these seven questions are given in the Appendix.

One more tip on improving your leverage—negotiate more important issues first. To some, this sounds logical. Get what you want out of the way as soon as possible. Others, however, feel that it is impolite or selfish to focus on yourself. Who says? Everyone knows that people look after themselves first, so don't go against human nature just to appear nice. If you are thinking this way, then you are probably a "Conflict Avoider"—and you shouldn't be negotiating in the first place. (See Chapter 11 for more on types of negotiators.) Leonardo da Vinci was quoted as saying, "It is easier to resist at the beginning than at the end." Remember this when it comes to negotiations. If you wait until the end to ask for what you want, then you are more likely to take good enough rather than hold out for what's best.

Personalities of a Negotiation

We know what a person thinks not when he tells us what he thinks, but by his actions.

— Isaac Bashevis Singer (1904–1991)

Not everyone is a ruthless negotiator. Many people love to haggle, but others avoid it at all costs. Understanding where on the spectrum your target is will help you with preparations—as well as countertactics should your negotiation turn ugly. Pace and Faules (1994) have the best definition of negotiation personalities I've seen, and rather than try to come up with something different but just as good, I'd like to highlight their definitions, adding some China-specific examples. They list these five negotiation personality types:

- Conflict Avoiders
- Accommodators
- Compromisers
- Problem Solvers
- Competitors

CONFLICT AVOIDERS

As the name suggests, Conflict Avoiders don't like to negotiate. In fact, that's the last thing they want. I see three reasons why someone would feel this way:

- Preferring goodwill to victory
- Seeing negotiation as a source of embarrassment
- Letting apathy rule

Preferring Goodwill to Victory

Someone once said "Winning isn't everything"—and many Conflict Avoiders take it for a motto, ignoring the rest of the statement that usually goes with it. For this group, maintaining goodwill and keeping everyone happy is more important than getting what's best for themselves. Often Conflict Avoiders fool themselves into believing that their target feels the same way. This was the case for Nadine (not her real name), a former senior manager for my company, back in June 2008.

It was time for our annual national team-building event, and Nadine had suggested we take everyone on our team to the historic city of Suzhou. "Everyone" was a big number—78 people in all, and the flights and train tickets alone were going to make this the most expensive team-building event we had ever done. Happily, however, Nadine had connections. She had befriended the general manager of Regalia Spa and Resort, who was interested in receiving bartered training for their new facility by the lake. From my place on the sidelines this sounded perfect, and I approved the deal. The deal got even better, when Howard Johnson, a neighboring hotel in Suzhou, agreed to a similar bartered deal. All accommodation for three nights and our awards ceremony dinner would be completely free!

Well, that was what Nadine thought. Two weeks before the team was scheduled to arrive, the Howard Johnson called Nadine to inform us that they had pulled out of their arrangement. No more barter deal; we'd have to pay the full value, as Nadine had never secured the agreement in writing. When she informed me I was understandably shocked. I knew that we had no time to find alternative accommodation for so many staff, and Nadine was extremely sorry.

"Make sure this doesn't happen with Regalia," I said, and she assured me that they had an agreement.

In business staff will make mistakes, and so I overlooked the Howard Johnson debacle as a learning experience. Furthermore, the Regalia proved to be a terrific location. Located on the Jin Ji lake and designed as a romantic getaway, the hotel was a great backdrop to host an awards ceremony dinner, and for me to spring a surprise proposal to the woman who is now my wife, in front of the entire team. The first evening, at the company awards ceremony dinner, the team looked amazing, dressed to the nines, and the next three days proved to be fun for all.

And then I learned the truth of the arrangement. Nadine did not have an agreement, or at least not one that was legally binding. She simply had e-mail correspondence between herself and the GM's assistant that was ambiguous regarding the details. "Fifty percent," they said, would be bartered. Nadine read it as "100 percent." She didn't have a clear contract, and in the end the credit card of another employee (who had offered to be a guarantor for what he thought would be a few bottles of extra wine) was charged.

Shortly after, Nadine showed clear signs that she was a Conflict Avoider. Instead of informing me of her mistake and demanding that Regalia honor the agreement as she understood it, she coerced our company's financial controller into cosigning a new contract agreeing to a 50 percent payment and 50 percent barter contract. She did this on behalf of the business, without her line manager's knowledge or approval, and in the hope that her relationship with the GM of Regalia could be retained. In this case maintaining goodwill was more important than winning, and also more important than her own job.

It's easy to think that all Chinese are born with the ability to negotiate, most often ruthlessly. After all, the stereotypical Chinese market seems full of shouting and insults. To the trained ear, however, this is a combination of overacting and the emphasis on Chinese words, which can sound rude, particularly the forth tone. In reality the path of least resistance is the road most often taken, and if that means giving in to keep the *status quo*, then so be it. Many Chinese would rather lose profit than their friendly reputation.

Seeing Negotiation as a Source of Embarrassment

The second reason someone could be a Conflict Avoider is that it is simply embarrassing to be caught up in an emotional argument. To such a person, asking for a discount feels uncomfortable. This pleases no one more than the salespeople in the clothing and souvenir markets in China, who routinely jack up prices for foreign tourists. These salespeople know that back in the tourists' home country asking for a discount is thought of as being cheap and therefore culturally unaccepted. Haggling is not a habit and so while tourists might initially try to negotiate the price down, most will soon feel uncomfortable and give in to the salesperson's demand.

That's what happened with Alice and Matt, two close friends from Australia who were visiting me back in 2007. On arrival at YaYa Show market, opposite the Workers' Stadium in Beijing, Alice and Matt had turned left while another friend and I had turned right. I assumed that they would scout for trinkets and then come back to me to help them with their negotiation. They did come back, but only after negotiating for a pair of Nike sneakers, for which they finally paid about US$44 (300 CNY). That sum proved to be US$35 more than the price I was able to negotiate for the same style of shoes from another vendor, and hardly the bargain that they were looking for. I asked Alice why she had accepted the price and she proved that she was a Conflict Avoider by telling me that they were "too embarrassed to negotiate." To make her feel better I told her to think of it as a US$7 pair of shoes and a US$37 tip to the salesperson.

Letting Apathy Rule

Apathy is the third cause of conflict avoidance. People in this category simply feel removed from the emotion of the negotiation and so give in because they just don't care.

This was the case for Shaun. According to Shaun, he was having a bad year. He's not the first person I'd met who blames everyone or everything else, including luck, for his circumstances, but he was the first whom I had employed with this condition. Life was out to get him, or so he felt, as he had been hospitalized twice within a two-month period, both times for getting injured in fights with locals. He escaped responsibility by telling himself he was a victim, but I soon found out that he was much to blame for his predicaments.

The first clue was when he got so drunk on the intercity train between Shanghai and Beijing, on the way to a team-building event, that he fell and cut his head. The irony of the occasion was known by all who rode with him, because he was the designated safety officer for the trip. The embarrassment was too much, and Shaun never arrived at the hotel. He went AWOL and returned to Shanghai ahead of his team. That was the beginning of the end for Shaun as an employee, as he began to miss scheduled training appointments without providing a reason. On his third no-show, I called him to give him his termination notice.

"Shaun, I have no idea what's gotten into you!" I said, failing to hide my anger. "You're a great trainer, but what you are doing is totally disrespectful to me and the team."

My blood was boiling as I tried to maintain control. I expected him to argue; to announce that someone else or some other thing was to blame. I expected the victim to reappear, but instead all I heard was apathy.

"I know. You are right. I am not the same guy I used to be. I'm falling apart."

His voice was a monotone. "I need to get out of here. I've got to get out of China."

"Right!" I said, as I felt my anger dissipate. "You should get out of here and take better care of yourself." Now my tone was turning to sympathy.

"Hang on," I thought. I'm meant to be angry at this guy, but it was impossible to be angry at a guy who didn't care about his job any more. He didn't want to argue about why he should keep his job, or how the world was to blame, not him. He had become apathetic about all that.

You may never meet a Shaun-like character in your company, but no doubt some of your sales staff have resigned in the past. When that happened, did you require them to give you a month's notice? If so, it's possible that you were creating apathetic short-term employees; people who negotiated with your clients half-heartedly at best from the moment they handed in their notice. My recommendation? If your sales staff are leaving, particularly to a competitor, first try to retain them for the long term (that is, prevent loss of your goodwill), but if that doesn't work, escort them directly off the premises. Of course you can still give them a hug good-bye, but don't risk having a Conflict Avoider in your midst.

Now, if you find that your target is a Conflict Avoider, understand that while it is tempting to take advantage of such people and bend them to your whim, your target may change in the future. In fact, your decisive victory may mean the target is out of a job, replaced by a better negotiator, or worse, it may inspire the target to retaliate after realizing what you've done. Better to keep people happy, at least a little. As the saying goes, "Keep your friends close, and your enemies closer." Chances are you'll be negotiating with the same target again sometime soon.

Finally, if the Conflict Avoider is a member of your negotiating team, then you have to pull that individual out of the negotiation. Conflict Avoiders are a liability. That applies to you too if you have just realized that you are a Conflict Avoider. You can't please everybody, and chances are that you'll lose your job if you don't fight for your company's best interests. The only time to be a Conflict Avoider is when you are stopped in an alley by an armed robber. Otherwise, it's better to fight rather than to give the other side just what they want.

ACCOMMODATORS

In my family my father is an Accommodator. Growing up in middle-class Melbourne, I can't remember a time when my dad wasn't waking up early on weekends to take me to "footie" practice, taking my Scout troop on adventures in the bush, or driving me back late from Judo classes. My childish ignorance took his love for granted, so dad, please know that I do appreciate what you did. That's the good side of being an Accommodator. But there's a bad side.

Accommodators value maintaining a relationship more than getting what's best for themselves, or what's best for those they represent. While my dad was "head of the family," mom definitely ruled the roost. Not that that was a bad thing all the time, but it meant that dad never stood up and pressured her to stop smoking—not even after grandma died of emphysema brought on by her own smoking habit. Mom eventually quit on her own, some 40 years after starting; no doubt because of the stigma of being a smoker, but not as a result of any pressure from dad.

As you might have gathered, being an Accommodator can be healthy for a family, but it doesn't put you in a strong position when it comes to business. So how do you know you're an Accommodator? If you find yourself saying to yourself, "I trust he will do the right thing," without actually asking him to do it, or if the best part of your day is listening to your colleagues in the lunch room and trying to solve their problems, then you are probably an Accommodator.

COMPROMISERS

Compromisers are similar to Accommodators in that they feel strongly about maintaining relationships with others. However, they are more balanced—like Yin and Yang. Mom cooks, and dad washes up. That's what Compromisers do. It's also the most common business negotiating style, because the result is deemed fair—50/50. Half for you, and half to them. It's almost perfect, but something is still missing. It could be better. What about 100/100? A strong negotiator can often find a settlement where both sides get all or most of what they really want, but you'll never find it if you say, "Oh, yeah, go ahead and take half."

PROBLEM SOLVERS

And that "better" is what Problem Solvers obtain. Rather than put up a sign to make drivers slow down on a particularly slippery-when-wet corner, scientists create a material that creates more, not less, grip when wet. Instead of relying on policing by convenience store operators, regulators make cigarettes so expensive that they are out of reach for underage smokers (and for my mom). Unfortunately, history shows that politicians rarely choose to problem solve. But you don't have to be a genius to do it. A bird and a cow are Problem Solvers. The bird sits confidently and well fed on the cow's back, pecking off ticks and insect lava, safe from predators on the ground.

In negotiations, Problem Solvers uncover the real need of the target and balance this with their own.

COMPETITORS

The United States is an obvious example of a Competitor. Most of the time the country gets what it wants, often due to its size or direct threats. Panama, Ecuador, Cuba, and Venezuela have all experienced negotiating with the United States as a Competitor.

Back in 1962 such negotiations almost ended in nuclear war, as Cuban leader Fidel Castro stood his ground, and the United States was slow to realize its defiant stance could result in its own destruction. Thankfully, President John F. Kennedy saved the day by being a Problem Solver instead. On October 14, 1962, a U.S. reconnaissance plane observed missile bases being built in Cuba. The crisis ended two weeks later, on October 28, 1962, when JFK and U.N. Secretary-General U Thant reached an agreement with the Soviets to dismantle the missiles in Cuba in exchange for an agreement never to invade Cuba. Castro's need to protect his country from an American invasion was met by the feature of a signed document from the U.S. president.

If you have two Competitors negotiating, you're in trouble. Neither wants to back down and be an Accommodator or even suggest a split like a Compromiser. Their only hope is for a mediator to introduce the concept of being a Problem Solver. Ah! If only it could be that easy.

CHAPTER 12

Tactics of Negotiation

The fellow who says he'll meet you halfway usually thinks he's standing on the dividing line.
— Orlando A. Battista (1917–1995)

The first rule of negotiation is to maintain a poker face. That is, when the target demonstrates a tactic, you do not react. Most tactics are designed to rattle you, to make you feel uncomfortable or even angry. Showing anything more than a smile will reduce your leverage as you will demonstrate an increased neediness by revealing your emotion. The best tactic in a negotiation is to first identify your target's needs and build goodwill to help reach mutually beneficial results. However, if a target is particularly troublesome, or you didn't have time to do your research and build rapport, then pay particular attention to each tactic's countertactic. And remember—should you choose to use these tactics against your targets—they may have read this book as well and know how to counter you.

IDENTIFY THE TACTIC

Your first task in a negotiation is to identify the tactic that the other side is using, so you can then prepare countermeasures. These are the 12 tactics that you're likely to see:

- Asking for a discount
- Moving the goalposts
- Offering pie in the sky
- Promising future business
- Playing good cop/bad cop
- Stonewalling
- Attacking
- Flinching
- Pleading limited authority
- Controlling the environment
- Invoking the power of numbers
- Being irrational

The following sections discuss each in turn, along with a countertactic.

Asking for a Discount

In China, before children learn arithmetic, they learn how to haggle. It is for this reason that the request for a discount is habitual regardless of whether you are negotiating the price of a pair of socks or a shipping container full of them. Now here's the kicker. It's also habitual to give that discount. Here's a typical negotiation:

"We are interested in buying 10,000 units of the RT789. Can we get a discount?"

"Sure. I can give you a 10 percent discount. How's that?"

"Can you give us 15 percent?"

"OK. 15 percent."

I've worked in China for eight years and am still amazed at how easy it is to negotiate lower prices, simply by asking. But before you say, "That only happens in small companies," let me inform you that I have used this technique with mainland China's largest building, the Shanghai World Financial Center (SWFC). As mentioned in Chapter 2, in March 2009, I arranged a public event titled Spark09. This event required three large rooms, and so I approached my former clients—the Forum at SWFC. As I had already built up goodwill, the "rack rate" of US$34,000 had already been slashed before negotiations really began. The quotation on the table for the Grand Hall and two conference rooms, however, was still significant, at US$11,000.

This is what I said:

"Thanks for the quotation. I was talking to my colleagues and we believe that the price is a little beyond our budget. Can you lower it?"

"OK. We can give it to you for 50,000 CNY. (About US$7,300.) How is that?"

Incredible! I got a 37 percent discount simply by asking. And this is just one case. The list of discounts that I have received over my time in China, just by asking, is in the hundreds. And sometimes I get discounts by accident. In one case, I was only window-shopping for laptops with a friend when a lightweight HP netbook caught my eye. As I approached, I noticed the sign listing the laptop's price at 5,000 CNY (about US$730), which I thought was reasonable. Turning to my friend I exclaimed in Chinese, "Cheap!" Only two years before I had paid twice that for a similar model. I was startled by the salesperson who suddenly appeared to my left as he announced, "Yes, I can make it cheaper! 3,500, OK?" I'm sure I did a double take as I realized I had involuntarily negotiated the price down by 30 percent. As I said, in China, offering a discount is habitual.

So what stops some people, particularly non-Chinese, from asking for a discount? The same reason the computer salesperson switched to automatic pilot when he heard the word "cheap," assuming I meant "Can you make it cheaper?" Social habit. In the West we don't haggle, and therefore we are not conditioned to ask for the discount. Our loss.

Countertactic

But what happens when you are the supplier, and the customer is asking you, "Can you provide us with a discount?" How do you avoid losing your margins as your Chinese sales team pacify the client and respond, "Sure. We can give you a 15 percent discount!" If you are the sales manager of a Chinese sales force, you need to recondition your team not to instinctively say yes to every request for a discount. Too many times, I have heard from my own sales team, "But they asked for a discount, and I didn't want to lose the contract." Lose the contract?! At this point in the relationship, you are unlikely to lose a contract over a discount, or at least not without significant warning. So what do your salespeople say to this request for a discount? Here's a selection of answers:

- "We'd like to give you a bigger discount, but this is the lowest price."
- "As you know, you've already received our best price."
- "I can certainly provide you with a further discount, if you pay up front/increase your order by 25 percent/commit to a two-year contract."

Notice how I imply that the customer has already received a discount. This is particularly important in China where the size of the discount is often more important than the overall price. Smart salespeople simply offer a higher initial price.

Moving the Goalposts

When someone moves the goalposts they are changing the conditions of the contract or verbal agreement, usually at the last moment, or even after the contract has been signed. Frustration, shock, and the feeling of unfairness overwhelm victims of this tactic, and because most times they are caught off guard, there is little they can do. Here's an example.

The Olympic Games were an amazing display of athletic performance. They also showcased some amazing negotiations, including negotiations held by the Beijing government with the *Today Show,* owned by NBC.

In the negotiation, the American negotiation team approached the Beijing government to secure filming rights at the Great Wall.

NBC's intention was to film a number of *Today* episodes on the wall, live, for the American audience, who were watching from 6 AM U.S. Eastern Standard Time. For this to happen, filming would occur at 6 PM, Beijing Standard Time.

The negotiation went relatively smoothly, although the American team went over their initial budget. However, as they had no BATNA (there is only one Great Wall of China) the increase was considered acceptable. On the morning of the shoot, the technical team began loading up their hired vans with the equipment. This included not only cameras, but lighting fixtures, cables, computers, TV monitors, backdrops, chairs, and desks. All told, three trucks and two 44-person buses were necessary. The U.S. negotiation team remained in their hotel to relax.

The Beijing government led the convoy through the city. Black Audis driven by police honked and flashed, warning drivers up ahead to make way. The *Today Show* people were pleased by their efficiency.

On arrival at the wall, the crew began the laborious task of unloading the trucks and assembling the outdoor studio. The weather was kind, and there was no sign of rain. But then the goalposts were moved.

A government official, one who had been present at the original negotiations and signing of the contract, approached the producer. He asked, through a translator, where the show's security personnel were. For a filming of this size, at least 12 guards were necessary before filming could begin. Everything must stop.

The *Today Show* team was frantic. In only a few hours the crew was supposed to be televising the show live to the United States, and now they were told that the wall was off limits. What's more, the original negotiation team had remained in the Beijing hotel, two hours' drive away.

With no BATNA and no experience in negotiating in China, the crew struck a deal. The local government, controlling that part of the wall, would provide security, and 12 guards miraculously appeared. So did an exorbitant fee.

The fact that goalposts can be moved even after contracts are signed is a reminder of the importance of goodwill. Ultimately, the more goodwill that you have with your target the less likely you are to be insulted with this negotiating technique. At the end of the day, a contract is only a piece of paper, and although it is legally binding, to enforce it you need lawyers, courts, witnesses, and a lot of time. It's unattractive to take action, and that is exactly why this tactic is used by the unscrupulous negotiator more often than you'd like to think. It's better to just be friends and avoid the whole kafuffle.

Countertactic

But what do you do if your target does move the goalposts against you? First, smile and stay silent. This will confuse the other side. After all, they have used this tactic to upset you, put you under pressure, and ultimately increase your neediness. But you won't let them see this, right? You will remain as cool as a cucumber.

Your second step is to remind the target of your goodwill, so you say, "Jin Bo, we've been working together for three years. I am sure you are not saying that you are changing the contract after you have signed it."

Notice the use of the statement, "I am sure you are not— rather than the question, "Are you . . . ?" You don't want to give the other person the opportunity to say "Yes." And of course you say this all with a smile.

And if that doesn't work, then your third technique is to remind the target of fairness. This third countertactic draws on research on what psychologists refer to as the "consistency principle." Possessing a high degree of consistency, as Robert Cialdini says in his book *Influence*, is associated in many cultures with personal and intellectual power. This is not the case in all cultures, but it is worth a try in China. Again, you need goodwill to use fairness as a defense. If the target has no interest in maintaining a future relationship with you, then appearing consistently fair is irrelevant.

Offering Pie in the Sky

This tactic starts with a highly inflated volume order. To date, the target has only ever ordered, say, 100 items per year, but now you have a request for more than 500 in the first month! This could be your big break, you think to yourself. Finally, all that hard work building good-will and reputation has paid off. It's almost too good to be true. As noted in the discussion of positive language in Chapter 5, words cause our unconscious minds to create images, if only for a few seconds or milliseconds, without our control. When the target says, "I'd like to order 500 items this month," you create an image in your mind, a vi-sion, of where you are going to be, financially speaking, with this huge order. You see yourself taking that well-earned holiday, driving that new car you've always wanted, or shaking hands with your boss to acknowledge a promotion. Even with the discount that the target requested, based on the increased volume, your company is going to make a huge profit. But then you notice that ringing in your head. Did someone set off the fire alarm?

It really is too good to be true, because this is a tactic—one that uses your unconscious mind against you. Don't think of a blue dog. You see, even this book can control your unconscious mind! Once the vision of success has been created, the target's next step is to crush your dream. This could be done a number of different ways, but most likely it involves informing you that the "head office has postponed the project for now," or that they are "having a cash flow problem cur-rently," so the order of 500 has to return to the original volume of 100. "Sorry about that," they say. "Oh, but we'd still like to keep the dis-count you gave us on the increased volume." You're in a pickle, and it is definitely sour.

Countertactic

If the target is sufficiently skillful, then you may even feel sorry for them. After all, it wasn't their fault that the order was reduced, was it? Remember, the target has probably been building goodwill with you, just so they would appear as much the victim when they pulled out the pie-in-the-sky card. So what do you do?

Step one is to tell yourself "Don't count your chickens before they're hatched" when a huge order lands on your lap. That maxim was coined for a reason. This is that reason!

Step two is to question the target's order as soon as feasible. You're not selling milk at the corner store, so you should know a bit about your customers' business and how your product or service is used by each organization. In Chapter 13, I discuss the importance of being able to add value to your targets' business. To be able to do this, you must understand their business processes intimately. Therefore, you should know well ahead of time if an increase in an order volume is plausible or not. So you say, "Hmmm, 500 seems like a lot. I've been talking with your (GM/production manager/sales director) and haven't heard anything about an increase in business. If you don't mind, please reconfirm the order and get back to me tomorrow."

It is better to be tough early on in the negotiation with the target. Again, as da Vinci said, "It is easier to resist at the beginning than at the end."

Promising Future Business

A popular tactic to push for lower prices is to say, "Hey, if you give me a discount today, I will introduce my friends to you" or "If you give me a discount today, then I will order more next month." This is baloney. The target will order more from you in the future because they are happy with your product or service as it matches a need, not because you give them a discount today. This is no more than a tactic, so remember that. If you really believe that if you don't give them the discount, they might leave, then your problem is that you have missed their need and haven't built enough goodwill.

I let one of my sales staff, who has since found other employment, make this mistake. Geoffrey is a stereotypical salesperson—hungry for the sale, but slightly disorganized. It took him awhile to realize that the "salesperson doesn't close the sale." Geoffrey successfully sold our Intensive Business Writing (IBW) course to the Shanghai office of Morgan Stanley. At first, the training manager stated that he wanted to "see first if we were suitable." That was understandable, but he also wanted a 25 percent discount. If this first contract was a success, the training manager said, he promised to increase the price for future training courses.

Sometimes you have to let your staff make their own mistakes, and so I agreed to Geoffrey's request to approve the contract. "It's going to be hard to increase the price back to the full 100 percent of value in the future," I warned. Geoffrey only smiled. He was just happy to sign with a Fortune 500 company.

Just over a year later, we have run 15 courses on a variety of topics with Morgan Stanley, but the price has remained the same. Furthermore, when the issue of raising the price was brought up, the target simply reminded us of consistency (see "Moving the Goalposts"). "We've been paying this price for a whole year, *so it's fair to keep it the same,* especially because of the economic crisis." Targets will always have an excuse why they should not pay more. You don't need a collapse in the sub-prime loan market, but that helps.

Countertactic

Don't rely on those promises! As the saying goes, "A bird in the hand is worth two in the bush." That is, don't leave success to chance; bank on what is before you, not what could be. Geoffrey should have said, "If we were a new business, I can understand your need to test us. However, we've been in the market for eight years, and we won 'Training Firm of the Year' in both 2007 and 2008. I am sure that you wouldn't ask a market leader to accept that sort of probation."

As with moving the goal posts, step one is to smile as you hold the line by saying something polite and firm. Don't destroy any goodwill that you've created by coming across as arrogant. Step two is to stop talking. Remain silent. That pause, to the point of being uncomfortable, will put your target on edge. If they don't blurt out something to reduce the tension first, you then say, "I am sure that you will be a repeat customer, because you will be completely satisfied with our service." You do not mention lowering of price.

Playing Good Cop/Bad Cop

This is a classic TV police show tactic, but it's worth describing the way it works off the screen. First, there is never a real *good* cop—a true friend to the target. The person playing this role is simply pretending to be good. It's an act, and designed to take advantage of the theory of reciprocity. The bad cop begins the negotiation, usually by offering the product or service at a ridiculously high price. You, the customer, balk, but before you walk away in disgust, the good cop wraps an arm over your shoulder and in reassuring tones, informs you that his colleague, the bad cop, is in a bad mood, and that you should ignore his behavior.

"I," announces the good cop, "will give you a reasonable price."

The good cop's price is lower than the bad cop's original price, but it is in no way reasonable. It's at least 10 to 20 percent above the market value. What happens next is purely unconscious. The rule of reciprocity kicks in again, and you have to fight yourself not to say yes. After all, this guy is helping you. Isn't he? You feel uncomfortable as you begin to feel indebted to him. You know you are uncomfortable for a reason, but you can't quite put your finger on it. Wait, now he's bringing you a cup of hot tea. What a nice man. Hmmmm, do they have this model in silver?

Countertactic

Understanding what is happening is your first countertactic. If you are caught unawares, then you can't consciously force your unconscious feelings down and acknowledge these two for what they really are; a strategic team. The next step, said with a smile, is to inform the two charlatans that you know what they are doing. Here's an example:

"Ha! I get it. You're the good cop, right? I guess that makes Mr. Angry over there the bad cop. Funny, I was watching *CSI New York* . . . "

Again, let me reiterate, do this with a smile. If you let yourself appear angry, you could embarrass or insult them, and they could withdraw any service, now and in the future.

Stonewalling

You've met these people before. They don't budge. No matter how much you push them to give you a discount or increase their offer, they refuse. "No," they say. "And that is my final offer."

I was negotiating with Yang Cheng (not her real name) from Lenovo in Beijing. We had previously agreed that I would undertake a day-and-a-half training course for Lenovo's HR department, but due to company structure changes I needed to stay in Guangzhou to support the team. My colleague Jeff agreed to take the training on my behalf, but Yang Cheng disagreed. She wanted me and me alone. I was touched by her commitment, but it was putting me out, big time.

There was also another catch. On one of the two days that she wanted me to train, I had already arranged meetings in Guangzhou, but Yang Cheng was stonewalling me. She was the decision maker for multiple Lenovo training courses, and if I handled this poorly, hundreds of thousands of yuan could be lost. Thankfully, I knew what to do.

Most stonewall standoffs result because one party doesn't truly know the needs of the other. "What are Yang Cheng's needs?" I asked myself. I didn't know, so I funneled her—all this via telephone. Within five minutes of talking I had uncovered her need. Yang Cheng, a young member of her HR department, was risk averse. The training that I had been booked for would be attended by her senior colleagues, and although Jeff was perfectly qualified to take my spot, she had already promoted the "GM of ClarkMorgan" as the trainer for the course. I saw my opening.

Knowing that I had to make an appearance, I proposed that the second day would be managed by my colleague Jeff. I would do the training, and Jeff would film the trainees in their final presentation. The proposition was accepted. I had scaled her stone wall.

Most stonewall confrontations are caused by a lack of information. So, when targets don't budge, you need to pause and uncover their needs through funneling. Otherwise you risk "negotiating with yourself"—changing your offer based on guesswork in ways that become less and less favorable to your interests. On Monday you call the client offering a price of, say US$1,000 per unit. They tell you that they will consider your offer and call you back tomorrow. But they don't. On Tuesday the phone doesn't ring, and you begin to worry.

"Maybe they are talking to my competitor," you ponder. So you pick up the phone and you call the target.

"Great news," you state confidently. "I can offer you a 10 percent discount."

The target says, "I'm happy to hear that," and then promises to call you tomorrow to confirm. They are pleased, and now so are you. You almost have the contract in the bag. The only problem is that when Wednesday comes your phone doesn't ring. Panicked, you call the target again.

"If you sign today," you state, "then I can give you a 15 percent discount." You can almost hear your own desperation. You can also hear the target smile through the phone.

"That sounds great!" they announce. "Let me call my boss and get back to you." But they never do. And why should they? After all, you are rewarding them for *not* calling you back. Each time they delay, they get a discount. How long can they keep you negotiating with yourself, they wonder. As long as it takes.

Countertactic

After identifying this tactic, consider several possible causes for the stalemate. Most likely, you haven't truly identified the target's need and are therefore trying to sell features that have no benefit to your target. Pause the negotiation and use your alternative sources of information to uncover the hidden need. Is the client risk averse? Is there an issue of saving face? Or is the target just focusing on positional negotiations? If it's a positional negotiation that you have found yourself in, one that focuses on the costs, then you have to change the game. Move to a needs-based negotiation.

Attacking

Attacks are more common when goodwill between parties is weak or repeat business is unlikely. However, an attack can also be launched from *mismatchers*—people who look for differences rather than similarities, and can often come across, at least at first, as aggressive (like my new Scottish friend in the Beijing pub).

Back in 2006, when my company still conducted business English training, Xiao Guan (not his real name), the HR manager for a major electronics firm, contacted my company to arrange a demo for his senior staff. Subsequently, Mike Joseph, one of our most experienced trainers and our national corporate training manager, conducted a demonstration class for a small group of company employees. The following e-mail (here reproduced word for word, spelling included) was received a day after the training demonstration:

Michael,

It is our pleasure to have this demo class.

The feedkack information from the attendees are:

Your attudite is very good;

Your Pronunciation is not as good as that "Kai En" American teacher;

What they want to study is English, but your company is focus on some other skill. That is not what they want. They wanto to study English. This is very important;

The training course arrangemnet and material is not as good as "Kai En." Maybe "Kai En" have more experience on English training.

Consider that you have good interpersonal skill, I sill want to consider you to the cycle. So we want to see your improve plan.

Best Regards,
Xiao Guan

On receiving the e-mail, the whole ClarkMorgan management were confused. If Xiao Guan believed that the Kai En trainer, training material, and overall company experience was better than that of ClarkMorgan, why were we still being considered? I sent an e-mail, highlighting the benefits of ClarkMorgan. The following e-mail (again reproduced exactly) was sent back from Xiao Guan:

How are you?

I would like bring an English training business to you. Do you like it?

We will have Business English training in Shanghai, Beijing and other office. [My company] is growing very fast in great China.

The condition to sign contract with your company Clarkmorgan is the quotation must below or equal RMB500.00/ Hour. That is what I can help you.

This company is a very big foreign company in China. I hope to help you. That is the compensation of GE chance.

I invited your people and your competitor "KAI EN" came to RA for demo training. After the demo, I give your people another chance to do demo again.

As you know I am very busy, I already try my best to help you. But the price must be lower or equal RMB500.00/Hour, though this price is still higher than your competitor. This price is the highest one that I can help you. It has no discussion!

Time is very urgent! You make the final choice. That is what I can help you, my old friend.

Best Regards,
Xiao Guan

For the first time, a value was added to the communication; "500 RMB/hour" (about US$80). This was significantly lower than the standard ClarkMorgan price. Instead of bending under pressure, I sent another e-mail similar to the last, highlighting the strengths of the company. The following e-mail was sent from Xiao Guan:

Hello,

I just receive a fax of your E-mail. It is a pity that you are too pride of yourselves. Like the E-mail, you just send it out like broadcast, Joseph does not care if the customer receives it or not.

I phone call you company again and again for the E-mail. I am quite tied be a customer of your company like this way!!!

To be a good friend of you and Molly, I really would like to help you. But it depends on you. I can not understand that Joseph even don't know how to talk with customer. It is your sales skill like this way?

Whatever I respect your choice, you make the final decision. I remember that Molly suggest that the foreign teacher will not come for the final test. It is a constructive suggestion. I did try my best to help you. But you can not help me convince my internal customer. You don't care about your friend and customer. It is a pity.

Best Regards,
Xiao Guan

The ClarkMorgan management were not sure of the next tactic. Xiao Guan was becoming increasingly unreasonable, and starting to use insults. We were unwilling to drop our price, as this would set a poor precedent. So what was our neediness level?

Cash flow and demand for ClarkMorgan were both very positive. In fact, business was almost double of the previous year. Our need for Xiao Guan's business was therefore low. As for ClarkMorgan's BATNA, if the negotiation didn't go ahead, the alternative would be to use the resources for another client, and we were already very busy. Therefore the BATNA was also very strong.

Xiao Guan's neediness was clear. He was currently looking for an English training vendor, and so his neediness was high. He had also stated in his second e-mail that he was "very busy" and that "time is very urgent," making the urgency to find a training vendor higher. Xiao Guan's BATNA was the big question. Did he really consider the competitor Kai En to be a suitable alternative to ClarkMorgan? The demonstration had been conducted on February 16, and the final e-mail was sent on March 7. If the training was very urgent, why hadn't he simply used his BATNA. Perhaps it was a bluff?

Xiao Guan was indeed bluffing. The account manager, Molly, signed the contract for 550 CNY per hour, which allowed for some discount, but was 10 percent higher than the 500 CNY (US$80) that Xiao Guan had demanded from the outset of the negotiation.

Countertactic

The key to counteracting an attack is not to react. Xiao Guan is an antagonist, and he uses this technique to get what he wants. This is the common trait of a mismatcher. When a mismatcher senses weakness they push even harder. The key is to smile and hold your ground.

Flinching

The flinch takes advantage of the unconscious human need to maintain the status quo and avoid causing pain to others. When Matt and Alice, my friends from Australia, came to visit me in 2007, I took them both to YaYa Show market to satisfy their craving for bargains. At four stories, this market offers almost everything anyone might want to buy, including knock-off Pierre Cardin ties, Columbia jackets, and UGG boots. The sheer volume of merchandise can be overwhelming, which is a dangerous state to be in when negotiating with seasoned salespeople.

Matt and Alice had little experience haggling, and, as mentioned earlier, were quickly fooled into paying six times the price for a pair of knock-off Nike shoes. Again, for the record, I was on the other side of the market then and wasn't involved in that initial transaction!

After learning that she had just paid an inflated price, Alice passed the task of buying a suitcase to me. With all the recent shopping she had done, she needed another suitcase to ship all her new clothes and DVDs back to Australia.

The conversation with the salesgirl in the suitcase stall went something like the following (translated from Chinese):

"How much for this bag?" I asked.

"How much do you want to pay?"

"You're the expert. How much for this bag?"

"OK. I will give you a good price because you speak Chinese. Six hundred CNY."

"Six hundred, eh? I'll give you three hundred CNY."

"*Aiya! Aiya!* (*Aiya* is the Chinese equivalent for "Shit!") That's too cheap! You want me to die? I can't eat with such a low price! *Aiya!*"

Countertactic

The salesgirl was screaming blue murder. Her face expressed pure agony. Her brow was furrowed. Her eyes showed glints of tears. This was a super flinch. All the while, I stood my ground, staring at her and not saying anything in response. She then ran out of things to say. She had used up all of her *Aiyas*.

Silence.

I smiled, and began to clap. "You are a movie star!" I said in Chinese, holding an imaginary Oscar in my hands and handing it to her. You could almost hear her face crack as it changed from agony to amusement to subtle embarrassment.

"Three hundred twenty," I added, "OK?" She said yes, and the deal was sealed. Her flinch hadn't beaten me.

Again, the key to counteracting the flinch is not to react. The second is to inform your target that you know what they are doing. I don't recommend that you embarrass them, as I did with the suitcase seller, but a gentle reminder that you know what they are doing will put them in their place, and make them realize that you are immune to their performance.

Pleading Limited Authority

"I'm not sure. Ask your mother." It's amazing that we still fall for the limited authority tactic, even though we've been hearing it since childhood. But there you are, sitting in the wedding shop, after picking out the wedding photo combination, and the salesperson says, "Oh. I'm not sure I can offer you this package for that price. I'll have to talk to my boss. Please wait a moment."

That was exactly what happened with a student of mine. His fiancée and he had already spent over an hour with the salesgirl, looking over extravagant wedding photo packages—a Chinese tradition in getting married. The price seemed too high, and so they asked for a discount—another Chinese tradition. The salesgirl disappeared for a few minutes stating that she needed to talk to the duty manager. "No one has ever gotten such a low price before," she added as she left.

A moment later, she returned. "I'm sorry," she said. "My manager says that's the best price." She had played the limited authority card.

Countertactic

Remember that neediness is increased with increased emotion and reduced time. The purpose of using the limited authority technique is to put pressure on the target (in this case you) by delaying the negotiation. If your time is limited, then your neediness begins to build, and therefore your leverage declines. You want to get out of there, and you don't want the last hour or so of negotiating to be a waste of time. You are therefore more likely to agree with the conditions. After all, her boss said it was the lowest price. But that is just another tactic; the use of authority to support the salesgirl's opinion. How do you know for sure if the duty manager is even here? You didn't see the salesgirl talk to him. Maybe she just made herself some tea instead.

So what do you do? You hold your ground. Remember that the same time pressure that they are trying to use against you can be used against them. When they inform you that their boss said no, then you calmly say, "I think it's best to see the manager in person." If the duty manager doesn't exist (that is, she really did make a cup of tea) then you will increase her emotion and therefore her neediness to sign the deal. If she looks uncomfortable, you add, "Or we can sign the contract now, based on my conditions."

If the duty manager does exist and joins the negotiation, then you simply demand the same conditions. Don't let the power of authority make you feel uncomfortable. The duty manager has probably only worked there a couple of years more than the salesgirl and is unlikely to be the owner.

Controlling the Environment

Making someone uncomfortable increases their emotion, and therefore their neediness. This can be done on a mental level, but it is much easier on a physical level. Keeping you waiting in the reception area for an extended period of time, turning the heat up or down depending on what you are wearing, or putting you into a lower seat are all physical ways to make you feel uncomfortable.

Countertactic

So what do you do when you realize that the air-conditioning is set at 59 degrees F. and you're beginning to feel the onset of frostbite, or the sun is streaming over your target's shoulder and straight into your eyes? Simple—move. By sitting there, uncomfortable, you are only going to make yourself more needy and signal your neediness to your target, which further weakens your leverage. If you don't want to be blunt, use an excuse to move. "Do you mind showing me to the break room? I'd love to get some coffee," you say.

Invoking the Power of Numbers

You were confident up until the point the door opened. Until then you thought the meeting was just going to include you and the target, but spread out in front of you, like Leonardo da Vinci's *The Last Supper*, must be every director from their company. A single bead of sweat runs down your face, and your heart goes into palpitations. You weren't ready for this!

I didn't have palpitations, but my palms definitely became sweaty during a similar incident a few years ago. Maggie, one of my account managers from our Beijing office, asked me to accompany her to meet the HR director of the Sheraton Great Wall Hotel. This was to be a general "get to know you" meeting, and so I was prepared for any number of random questions. I just wasn't ready for every director being present. Apparently, our meeting had been scheduled as part of their half-yearly directors' meeting. Not knowing who I should address as my target and feeling under pressure from the eight pairs of eyes staring at me, I stumbled through the meeting, and left feeling as if the whole experience had wasted all of our time. Had I been mentally prepared and less nervous, I would have reacted differently. They had successfully controlled my emotion, and therefore my neediness.

Countertactic

The best way to combat this tactic is to avoid it. Make sure you know how many people will be attending the meeting prior to leaving your office. If the answer is eight, then don't go alone, take at least another two colleagues.

Being Irrational

Acting crazy during a negotiation is a rare tactic, and would probably work better for getting out of a street fight than for negotiating an import duty. Nevertheless, it is a tactic that appears occasionally in business, and therefore you should have a countertactic.

I found myself having to fall back on my own advice during the last few months of 2008. In hindsight it's clear that James was a terrible hire, but at the time of his employment, at the beginning of 2008, we thought we needed a financial controller to keep an extra pair of eyes on costs as we grew from 50 to 85 staff. James had been born in Shanghai, but he had the demeanor and vocabulary of a 19th-century British explorer. He had earned his master's in Bath, England, and had obviously picked up more than a degree there. I just thought his oddity came with being an accountant.

In July, his oddness became disturbing. A botched negotiation with a five-star resort meant that we were faced with a large, unplanned expense, and our financial controller had tried to sweep it under the rug, possibly due to the loss of face that it could bring. He received his first written warning.

It was at that point that I started to realize that James was incredibly irrational. He had been recording our mobile phone conversations, and had tried to frame the said five-star resort, even going as far as forcing a new intern to assist him in his underhanded act. All the while, he believed he was doing nothing wrong.

James was eventually asked to leave, but that wasn't the end of it. Earlier that year, the Chinese government had introduced new employment legislation that to this day has caused more than headaches for businesses employing underperforming staff. Three bilaterally signed written warnings were now required, and the cause for the dismissal had to be incredibly wrong, to the point of being some illegal act on the part of the employee. James, with a background in law, knew he could push. And he did.

I've always joked that China is a small country. Sure, there's 1.3 billion people, and if a city doesn't have more than 5 million people, it is considered small. But in business here, names and faces reappear, particularly because many people only rotate among the foreign-invested enterprises, which are obviously few in relation to all the businesses in China. Regardless, I have seen employees, both from my company and those of my friends, burn bridges when they leave their employer. Whereas in Australia a positive reference from a previous line manager is vital to a successful employment transition that same belief may not be held as strongly in China. I assume this is mostly due to the past double-digit growth in GDP, which has generated a higher demand for talent than the current supply.

So there I found myself, negotiating with an intelligent and well-informed employee who had just received his marching orders and resented it. This was more than a monetary issue. There was clearly a loss of face.

James was clearly emotional—and unfortunately his irrationality was indeed real! This was confirmed when I opened my e-mail inbox to see the following sentence, "Now you totally should pay me RMB 47,748 [US$6,800]. If you choose to settle it within 3 days (by 1200 hrs 20th November) together with a formal apology, I will refrain from taking the aforementioned actions." Those aforementioned actions included clear threats to close the company. So what did we do?

Countertactic

First, you have to consider whether your target actually is crazy. If they are, then you should ask yourself, "Should I be negotiating with this wacko?" You should have a BATNA, so perhaps you should consider your second option. If you suspect that this is just an act, then, as with an attack, you should sit there calmly and not react. All the target is trying to do is increase your emotion and hence your neediness.

As with all tactics, the key is not to react. James was obviously irrational, and the risk with irrational people is that they are willing to lose everything to prove a point. That would simply be lose-lose for both of us. However, at the same time, we didn't want to give in to his demands. It was time to increase his neediness, so we delayed.

At 12 noon on the 20th of November, James did not receive a phone call from us, in order to settle the account. At 12:01 ~PM he sent an angry SMS message: "Because my request has not been responded positively by 1200 hrs today, I will have to be taking actions." I waited until 12:45 before I gave him a call. By doing this, I knew that his emotion, and hence neediness, would be high. He had set a deadline, and I had ignored it—intentionally. Deadlines are used by the target to increase your neediness, so do your best not to react to them.

James almost screamed down the phone. He was understandably livid because I knew he hated to be out of the control seat. By ignoring his threat, I had essentially shown that I wasn't worried, and therefore had more leverage. In reality I knew he could turn vicious, and that that was the reason I called—to calm him down.

While he shouted threats, I kept my tone and volume at normal speaking levels. He would jump on any emotion that I showed, so I was very careful. I also stated that as I was in Guangzhou, and not in the HQ in Shanghai, and so I couldn't confirm his demands today.

"James," I said. "I've appreciated your work, and believe you should be compensated fairly. We should be working toward a true win-win situation. The entire team would feel terrible if they knew that their jobs were threatened because of a misunderstanding."

I was careful not to blame James, and so I used passive sentences. My goal was to make him realize his actions could ultimately damage his relationship with others, rather than with me. It was clear that he didn't care about our relationship. This was important because it was clear that his need in his negotiation was related to saving face. The conversation finished, and I promised to get back to him in another 24 hours. When we finished the conversation he was much calmer, and I had broken his stone wall. I had also added more time in my favor, and was therefore increasing his neediness and thus my overall leverage. The next day I didn't call. Instead my business partner Andy, sent an e-mail:

James,
There needs to be an equal energy exchange between us and rather than attempting to destroy us, let's turn the energy around. Here is how it is going to work.

Andy then outlined how James was going to come to a colleague's home, where we would finalize his termination payout. He then added a radical request.

Over the coming days while you look for a new job, you will also do some project work for us from home.

The request was purely a tactic, as we were sure that James would want to get the money and run. However, this request for further help would unconsciously create the impression that we were on his side, while feeding his need to save face. It worked. James left our last meeting US$4,300 richer, and we avoided a legal headache while saving US$2,500. His irrationality was beaten by first not reacting, then controlling deadlines, and finally finding needs and meeting those needs.

Forewarned is forearmed, as the saying goes. Simply being familiar with these tactics should allow you to avoid falling for them most of the time.

Part Four

Keeping Your
Target Satisfied

CHAPTER **13**

Maintenance

*Men keep agreements when it is to the advantage of neither to
break them.*

—Solon (638–559 BC)

B eware! Just because the contract has been signed, and the target
took you out to dinner to celebrate your future cooperation, it
doesn't mean that things will go smoothly. A business arrangement is a lot like a marriage—and just as in a marriage, you must
maintain the relationship. This chapter discusses how.

SHARING INFORMATION

I live on the ground floor of a low-rise apartment complex in Shanghai
with my wife and son. I chose it because I can look out at trees, instead
of at other buildings and cosmopolitan smog. Many Shanghai residents
don't like the first floor because it can be damp. It also sees a higher
number of mosquitoes and creepy-crawlies in summer. As for the
dampness, I'm not bothered, because I have a diligent maid who wipes
the windows of condensation each day, and as an Australian, I quite
like living close to nature. And on rare occasions, even insects can
teach you about life!

One lazy Sunday afternoon I spilled Coca-Cola on the kitchen counter. Here's the scene. I'm darting from fridge to glass cupboard holding a two-liter bottle as I call out to my wife who still sits before the TV, "What's happening?" Apparently something good, because I slopped the Coke onto the counter as well as into the glass and rushed back without cleaning up the mess. An hour later, when the movie was over, I returned to the kitchen to find a line of ants marching to the pool of liquid sugar and then back again—back to their nest, presumably. And all this coordination in under an hour!

Now ask yourself, if faced with a business opportunity as rich as my spilled Coke was to those ants, could your company or department muster the resources necessary to take advantage of the situation, move, and collect. Could a single employee in your organization trigger sales, operations, and logistics in the time it took for the credits to roll on my movie? Chances are it would take much longer than an hour. Perhaps as much as a week or more, but there they were, a horde of tiny, simple creatures reacting as one and reaping the rewards. They were following the TALK principle! *TALK* stands for "tell," "ask," "listen," and "know." I created it back in 2006 in response to being frustrated with staff members working alone and not thinking for themselves. The tipping point occurred during the setup of a social networking event for our KIIs and targets at Number 5 Bar on the Bund in Shanghai. I was setting up a large banner—two meters by two meters—with colleague Jeff Lunz when my sales team arrived. I was surprised to see that they were all empty-handed instead of loaded with detail pieces and marketing collateral. When I asked the most senior saleswoman, her response shocked me. "Nobody told us!" she said in defense. This was at least the tenth event of this nature that we had done. Hadn't they realized by now? I exploded, and instantly regretted my reaction. The sales team was demotivated only minutes before the first of 60 or so customers were to arrive. There had to be a better way to create change than screaming after a problem surfaced, I thought, and that's why I developed TALK. Looking back at that moment, I see that TALK would never have been born without some pain. But now, I teach this acronym to managers around China, and once it is taught to a small number of staff it quickly reaches critical mass and changes company culture. Here's the breakdown.

Tell

The tell step encourages you to share your thoughts and information. Nothing is too trivial with tell. As you pass people in the break room you'll also pass on some business news you think might be of relevance. With tell everyone becomes a conduit for information, allowing news to travel fast. Note though, that tell is not gossip or hearsay. It's information that the other person might find useful. For example:

- "Bill, my friend Sam works for a TV station and she's looking for an expert on import tariffs to interview. Maybe you'd be interested."
- "Wangwei, I was just in the storage room and noticed that you are down to your last batch of marketing brochures. You might want to speak to the receptionist about ordering more."

Another way to tell is via MSN Messenger, Yahoo Messenger, or Skype accounts. These three instant messaging programs allow you to announce where you are and what you're doing with an editable field under or beside your name. For example, when I'm in Beijing—say, training Pfizer—my MSN Messenger account reads:

Morry: Mon/Tue Pfizer Neg. Skills. Free Wed-Fri for meetings.

Everyone in my company can see quickly where I am, and don't need to call me to find out. As my staff arrange my time for meetings, they can plan ahead without my involvement, and book me for meetings from Wednesday through to Friday. All because I tell.

"But my company doesn't allow MSN," I hear you say. This is a common trend around the world, as managers blame technology for lack of engagement, rather than their own management and motivation skills. Do you think Microsoft bans MSN? Of course not, and it seems to be doing just fine. If you're going to ban MSN because you're afraid staff will abuse this tool and chat with friends, you might as well ban SMSing or the mobile phone as well.

Ask

I blew my top when my senior saleswoman responded with "Nobody told us!" After I calmed down I vowed that I would never hear those words again. That's the role of ask. If you don't know, ask. If you forget, ask. If you forget again, ask again. The idea of ask is to make it clear that it's OK to ask any number of times and nobody can say, "I already told you!" Why? Because of the tell in TALK. And ask also means that you, or anyone in your organization, can't escape responsibility by saying, "Nobody told me!" Why? Because you or they should have asked! Tell and ask go hand in hand.

You might think that giving staff the option to ask an unlimited number of times reduces responsibility, because it allows staff to keep forgetting. But it doesn't work that way. First, if you've hired staff who can't retain information, then you've got an HR issue. And second, think back to the time when you were a new employee, green, and absolutely frightened that you'd say or do the wrong thing. Each day you'd edge your way up the learning curve, trying to understand the new jargon, processes, and everyone's names. Imagine if the place had had no veil of paranoia, so you could ask questions without a care. How fast would you have learned the ropes? And how much more efficient would the workforce be?

Listen

In our modern world, with mobile phones, SMS, and instant messaging, it's easy to forget our manners when talking face-to-face. No doubt you've been in a meeting when someone's mobile phone has rung. Perhaps they even answered it. Even worse, they started a conversation while you sat there, mouth open, ready to finish the sentence that was cut off by the incoming call. You may have even witnessed the call recipient stand up, leaving you alone in the meeting room, pondering the length of your fingernails. All these scenarios are simply bad form.

Listen is a reminder that the person before us deserves our full attention. Mobile phones go to silent, laptop lids are lowered, or chairs are turned away from the computer screen to face the speaker. Lack of attention equals lack of respect.

Listen also calls for *active listening*. This means that you make eye contact, nod at the right moments, and say things like "Oh, I see" and "Right" so the talker knows you are listening. You might even summarize, in your own words, what is being said, to clarify and confirm understanding. And as "communication is the response you get," use open questions with the listener to ensure you're understood. For example, say something like this: "So that I know I've been clear, please tell me the date and address of the next marketing event."

Know

If you "T," "A," and "L," then you will *know* what is happening in your organization, and know what opportunities are present. Know allows your organization to function much more efficiently, and moves the role of knowledge sharing from the few to the many. Knowing is how those ants were able to take advantage of the Coca-Cola within an hour. Knowing is what made their "organization" prosper.

In order to get TALK practiced within your organization, senior management must start using the lingo in their daily communication, whether that is spoken or e-mail. For example:

- "I'd love to talk about import tariffs. Thanks for TALKing."
- "Thank goodness you TALKed. I almost forgot to order new brochures. I'll do it now!"

My company's IT manager, Mark, demonstrated TALK just this year, when he informed me of a spelling mistake in our advertisement for a free public training course in Hong Kong. The trainer had missed the mistake, the regional sales manager had missed the mistake, and also the general manager (Morry Morgan) had missed the mistake. It was certainly not in the IT manager's job description to proofread marketing materials, particularly because he is not a native English speaker, but his TALK was much appreciated.

Encourage making TALK part of your company culture by placing signs around your workplace. Sharing of information is often against a salesperson's nature, and this is even more accentuated in the

Balinghou generation, who were brought up under the "One Child Policy" and aren't really used to having trusted people to talk to, so be sure to add it to your company handbook and point it out as a virtue that will be considered when promotions are to be awarded. In my company we present the "TALK Award" to staff who have demonstrated it in action, and since this acronym became part of our company culture, communication has improved exponentially. And, most important, "nobody told me" has been banished.

CALL, DON'T E-MAIL, THROUGH PROBLEMS

Problems are bound to arise between you and your target during the period of the contract. Late delivery, quality issues, or operating cost increases could require some form of modification to the contract. Don't send e-mail—it's too cold. You are likely to receive a legal notice in return. Instead, make a phone call, or even better, visit the target to discuss the problem face-to-face.

During the financial crisis in 2008, I had to deliver bad news to my staff. Clients were delaying payment and contracts had been postponed, wreaking havoc on our cash flow. Projections showed that we were unlikely to be able to pay the entire team on the fifth of the next month. Instead of sending out a company-wide e-mail that could have caused a mass exodus or mutiny, I called or spoke in person to every person in the company. It wasn't quick. It took almost an entire week, but the result was that we maintained morale, avoided an internal crisis, and made all the employees feel important.

Of course, this isn't so easy when you are on the other side of the world from your target. China is eight hours ahead of London and 12 hours ahead of New York, making this rule easier to proclaim than to follow. However, you'll be surprised how many people, and not just the Chinese, resort to e-mail as their first choice, even when their staff are situated in the same city. As English is often the business language between vendor and supplier, this reluctance can be due to weak spoken English ability. If that's the case, call "Wall Street English" school or one of its competitors and get them some training.

OFFER SOLUTIONS

I was leaving the Regalia Resort in Suzhou, Jiangsu Province, with a lot of baggage. The night before, my company had carried out a team-building and training event, and somehow I was now responsible for moving 80 marketing folders to the next destination, on the other side of the city. The concierge thought I needed a taxi, and I concurred.

"Take a seat," he said, after calling the taxi company. "The taxi will be here in 15 minutes."

Fifteen minutes later a small taxi arrived. It was clearly too small to carry my colleague, myself, and the five boxes of marketing material.

"I'm sorry," said the concierge, as he walked up to me. "The taxi is too small."

"I can see that," I responded. I was curious to see how he would handle this.

"OK," he said. His facial expression suggested that he had done all he could do.

"OK?" I asked. "What do you want me to do, live in this hotel indefinitely?"

There was a pause. The concierge was now considering his options.

"How about you get me a bigger taxi?" I added after almost 10 seconds of silence.

Flash!

"Yes! I will order a bigger taxi!" he stated happily, as if we had just stumbled across a scientific breakthrough.

He ordered a taxi, but the image of the five-star hotel had been damaged by his incompetence. He should have had a standard operating procedure (SOP) for such a simple, and probably common, problem.

ADD VALUE (THINK LIKE YOUR TARGET)

Offering solutions to problems that arise is one thing; providing solutions to problems that haven't come up yet is another. Thinking like your target is a great way to add value to your relationship. Instead of waiting to be asked to solve a problem, use foresight.

That might mean subscribing to magazines that would be read by your targets, attending networking events that are perhaps more relevant to your target than to your own business, or simply scrolling through discussions on LinkedIn and other web-based discussion forums. My company goes a step further with the publication of our own human resource magazine, *Network HR*, which discusses benefits and remuneration, recruitment, and, of course, training, as well as other issues relevant to the human resource industry.

MAINTAIN GOODWILL

Having the highest level of goodwill is how you get the contract signed in the first place. But don't forget to maintain that goodwill. If goodwill is damaged between you and your target, your contract could begin to unravel. This is where a good CRM program is useful. Record birthdays, interests, and kids' names, and keep checking the target even after they have bought. Any good salesperson knows that repeat business is many times easier and cheaper than new business to obtain.

Even after you follow these five steps to the letter, chances are you will still need the next chapter—how to handle complaints.

CHAPTER **14**

Handling
Complaints

Your most unhappy customers are your greatest source of learning.
—Bill Gates (1955–)

ven if you're doing everything right, you will still occasionally get
a complaint. How do you feel when you hear a complaint? Probably one or more of the following:

- Upset
- Embarrassed
- Angry

All these are negative feelings, and that's why everyone hates to
get complaints. These negative feelings are created by conditioning
over many years. But what if I could change that? What if I could
make you feel happy about receiving a complaint? I think that is possible, if you understand what is going on.

WHY DO CUSTOMERS COMPLAIN?

I live in Shanghai, and because the traffic is chaotic and borderline
dangerous, I choose not to drive. Back in 2008, the American news

station CNN reported that while China has 2 percent of the world's cars, it has 15 percent of the world's car-related deaths. That's what I mean by dangerous. Oh, and there's also a significant disproportion of cars to parking spaces. So instead of driving myself, I use taxis; a necessary evil in my eyes, because their drivers add to the dangers of the road. They speed, run red lights, almost run down pedestrians and cyclists, and practically take corners on two wheels, causing you to slide across the back seat (which never has seat belts).

One afternoon I took a taxi to the Shanghai Hongqiao Airport for a flight to Beijing. Looking out the window of the cab, I realized that we had passed the turnoff from the elevated highway. The driver noticed this at the same time, and in an incredible act of stupidity he braked heavily, stopping us in the middle of a three-lane highway. Stunned, I shouted for him to keep driving, but he ignored my pleas and instead grabbed the gear stick, putting the car in reverse! Now you understand why I call taxis in China an evil, if a necessary one.

However, the point of this story is not to highlight the incompetence of taxi drivers, but rather to bring up the fact that although I've been subjected to countless instances of poor service, I've never officially complained. I've shouted at the drivers, and in the "reversing down the freeway incident" I dare say I used some of my more colorful Chinese vocabulary, but I have never written a letter or called a hotline to record my complaint. If you've ever lived in Shanghai, or any big city around the world, then you are probably the same. Why is this? Here's what you probably said:

- "Nothing will change if I complain."
- "With over 40,000 taxis in Shanghai, the chance that I will meet the same taxi driver again is unlikely."
- "I'm too busy to complain."

So if a near-death experience at the hands of a taxi driver doesn't cause you to pick up the phone or write an e-mail, what does? The answer is loyalty. All three responses to why one does not complain fall under the same concept—you are not loyal. Loyalty is what makes us complain, or makes us move our business elsewhere. So who does complain? Loyal people complain. This changes everything. Instead of feeling negative emotions the next time you receive a complaint, you should be happy. After all, you have just identified a loyal customer who is willing to stick with you as long as you make improvements. That's why, as Bill Gates says, "Your most unhappy customers are your greatest source of learning."

Of course, loyalty isn't discovered from receiving complaints alone. It can be developed from a long-term relationship with a target, but how long does it take before you can consider someone a loyal customer? Perhaps you could assume that a customer was loyal at, say, three years. But maybe that's not enough. One of our customers, Nortel, had been using our services for three years, but when we changed account managers, we lost the goodwill we'd built up, and two months later Nortel dropped us. They weren't loyal after three years, so maybe your three-year-old customers aren't either. Could they be loyal after five years, then? The point is that it is very, very difficult to determine whether a client is loyal or not, unless you personally know their CEO. But with a complaint, you know instantly, because loyal people are the ones who complain.

You may recall the uproar in 1985, when Coca-Cola introduced New Coke in the United States. "Old Coke" drinkers protested en masse, and the Coca-Cola headquarters received more than 60,000 complaint phone calls. These angry targets complained because they wanted to continue to drink "original" Coca-Cola rather than switch to New Coke, which they saw as imitating Pepsi. That same year they got their wish. Original Coke was back.

Of course, this doesn't mean that a target is loyal from choice. It is possible that some of your targets have "forced loyalty." Here's an example:

I was having lunch with the general manager of Holesworth & Vose (H&V) and his team in the Eastern Chinese city of Suzhou, following a sales and negotiation training course. The H&V factory is based in the China-Singapore Suzhou Industrial Park, and so the choice of restaurants within walking distance was limited. Limited to one. During the meal, the GM informed me that while he and his colleagues frequent this restaurant each week, the wait staff always forget to bring the rice at the beginning of the meal, regardless of how many times they are reminded. He continued telling me that he also complains about this every time he comes, but alas, the management has changed nothing. Nonetheless, the GM and his team continue to come back, but only because of their forced loyalty. They're loyal, not from choice, but because it is the only restaurant within walking distance. This restaurant can continue to forget the rice, that is, until another restaurant opens within walking distance. At that point its loyal H&V customers will vanish.

THE FIVE STEPS TO COMPLAINT HANDLING

So now that you know that customers who complain are loyal, how should you respond to their complaint? Well, it's good news that those customers who complain are loyal, so obviously the first step is to say thank you.

Thank the Target

Hang on! Shouldn't the first thing you say be "I'm sorry"? No—"sorry" is of less importance to an angry client. The most important thing is to move them away from feeling angry, and so the first words they need to hear should be positive. Few words are more positive than "thank you," and we have been conditioned to respond to them with "you are welcome." Therefore, by saying thank you, you are reframing the target's bad experience into one that is positive.

Many of us are also sick of hearing staff say "Sorry, sorry" and then receiving no solution or improvement. Consequently, many people have come to associate the word *sorry* with a feeling of frustration. That's why you should start by saying thank you. For example:

- "Thank you for bringing this problem to my attention."
- "I didn't realize that there was a lead time issue, so thank you for highlighting this."
- "Thanks for helping us improve our business."

Talk About the Past

Next, remind the target of your previous positive relationship. No matter if the customer is new or a long-term user of your product or service, remind them that they have been satisfied in the past. After saying "thank you," say something like this:

- ■ "I've seen your face in our restaurant before, so you must have been happy with the service and food in the past."
- ■ "Our businesses have been cooperating for the past five years, and we've always received positive feedback from your salespeople."

Like saying "thank you," reminding targets of their previous positive experiences will put them in the right frame of mind and reduce tension.

Talk About a Current Solution

As noted, saying "sorry" is useless to a target, particularly if there is no solution. So, after saying "thank you" and reminding the target of their past satisfaction, you quickly inform them of what steps you are taking to fix the problem and ensure that it will never happen again.

- ■ "I've sent your concerns to my quality control manager, and he will respond by the end of the day."
- ■ "I have a meeting scheduled with my sales manager in 15 minutes to discuss your specific concern."
- ■ "Our operations manager is looking at this problem right now, and will let me know how to correct this by 4 p.m. today."
- ■ "I can offer you a 10 percent discount on this order right now."

If you don't tell unhappy targets what you are doing to solve the problem, they will continue to feel frustrated.

Talk About the Future

Once you have said thank you, highlighted your past positive relationship, and told the target what you are going to do to resolve the problem, it is time to talk about the rosy future that continuing cooperation will bring:

- ■ "I am sure you will be satisfied with the action we will take to resolve the problem, and will continue to use us in the future."
- ■ "I am looking forward to seeing you back in the restaurant next week."
- ■ "I know that your procurement team will be happy with this solution, and we'll be able to prepare next month's order."

Arrange a Meeting for Future Sales

Very few sales are ever made over the phone or by e-mail. A meeting, face-to-face, is vital to secure more business, and receiving a complaint from a loyal customer is a perfect opportunity to ask for a meeting with your target. Remember, they are loyal and want to continue to use your business in the future.

In 2007, my company provided business English training for an American elevator company in Zhangjiang Gao Ke, the Silicon Valley of Shanghai. At the conclusion of the six-month course, the manager, Lily (who had signed the initial contract), informed me that she was not 100 percent satisfied with the results of the course. Her staff had had so many work commitments that most of the weekly classes were less than half full, and she saw little benefit from the training.

She had a valid complaint. Maggie, my company's manager working on the contract, had given the Lily everything that she wanted, but in hindsight, it was clear that it wasn't what Lily had really needed. Maggie had made the mistake of taking the "customer is always right" too literally, and hadn't provided her own expertise. Lily should have been sold intensive courses that would have fitted better into her staff's busy schedule. I knew this, and so I followed the five steps over a phone call with Lily and finished by asking to meet with her the next week.

The meeting could not have gone better. An hour later, our goodwill had been restored, and Lily informed us that she believed our company had the best reputation in the market. Our trust score was once again high. It was at this point that I proposed further training, based on the new information that Lily had provided, and she agreed. She also went a step further, asking to receive a comprehensive proposal within the month. Her need for a speedy negotiation was clear from her words and also from her appearance—she was wearing a maternity dress.

Now that you understand the five steps to handling a complaint, here's a sample e-mail:

> Dear Mr. Wang,
>
> Thank you for informing us of quality issues regarding our latest shipment, #1234.
>
> Your comments are very important to us, as we have been working together for over five years, and during that time you have been satisfied with our quality.
>
> However, we will be correcting our process to ensure that this mistake does not happen again, and that you can continue to receive high-quality products in the future.
>
> In fact, I am so sure that you will be satisfied that I'd like to introduce a number of new products that we will be launching next month. Please let me know if you are free next Wednesday and I will visit your factory.
>
> Best regards,
> YOU

Now, the next time you receive a complaint you will not feel upset, embarrassed, or angry. You will feel happy, because you have just confirmed a loyal customer and you have an opportunity to gain more business.

Part Five

CHAPTER **15**

Execution

Vision without execution is hallucination.

—Thomas Edison (1847–1931)

Only one thing is more frustrating for a trainer than trying to hunt down a whiteboard marker that hasn't dried up, and that is returning for a follow-up class to find that the trainees' memories are in the same state. The whole training feels like I am "playing in front of cows" (对牛弹琴; *duì niú tán qín*). That is, a useless exercise.

All the theory in the world means little if it is committed to a trainee's RAM—and then deleted with the reboot of a new day. The new skills, or vision, as Thomas Edison said, are simply hallucinations if not used, so it's necessary to use them even if you stumble at first. It took me 15 years to develop the contents of this book, and I definitely tripped up many times on this journey. Don't be afraid of making these mistakes. Paul Galvin, founder of Motorola, told his son, Bob, when preparing him to take over the company, "keep the company moving"—even though any movement is bound to result in a stumble now and again.

This was the message that I told my staff at the national team-building event in Suzhou in July 2008. Months earlier I had changed the company motto from the very generic "Your Training Partner" to the more meaningful "Evolving People." The marketplace was changing, and this new motto was a message for both my targets and my own staff. They needed to evolve, keep moving, so that they were not left behind. In that presentation I asked my staff to consider if they were still evolving in their job, and if not, to ask themselves why not?

"If it's because you believe that you have 'arrived,' then congratulations. You are the corporate equivalent of the Dodo, the Tasmanian Tiger, and the 5 1/2 inch floppy," I said with intended sarcasm. I went on to say that I expect ClarkMorgan employees to believe that there is no finishing line, that they are in perpetual motion, learning from others, publications, and their own experiences. Less than six months after that speech the global financial crisis swept over the world, wreaking havoc with the training market and causing us to make heavy cutbacks on staff numbers. Those who had listened and evolved were not left behind, and I now expect the same from you. As a salesperson you now have the tools, the stories, and the evidence from my success, and now all you have to do is keep the knowledge in the front of your mind and use it. Don't retire this book to the bookshelf. Rather, make sure it escorts you on your next sales meeting or negotiation, and use it as a reference guide.

If, on the other hand, you are a sales manager and plan to use the advice from this book to completely overhaul your sales process, let me give you a final piece of advice. The New Year in the West acts as a mental "reset button," allowing new ideas and processes to be introduced from January 1 onward. In China this reset occurs after Chinese New Year. As Chinese New Year is based on the lunar calendar, this means that your revamp could begin anywhere between mid-January and late February, depending on the year. Whenever it occurs, right after the Chinese New Year is a great time to introduce this book and its concepts to your team.

Now use it or lose it, and go out and get those targets!

Appendix

British Council versus Virgin Atlantic Negotiation:

- Assuming you are the British Council, what concerns might Virgin Atlantic raise at your meeting?

Answer: Virgin Atlantic would probably want to know whether the event is exclusive, or if other airlines have been invited. As they have already cooperated in the past, they know that around 300 to 500 targets have attended, but they would probably like to know how the British Council is going to guarantee similar numbers.

- What kind of information is currently unknown to you?

Answer: The British Council doesn't know if Virgin Atlantic has been doing well that year or if business has been poor. If business was poor, then the airline has a higher need for promotion. Also, the British Council doesn't know if there are any changes to the immigration law in the United Kingdom. Any changes would seriously affect ticket sales, either positively or negatively.

- Who has stronger leverage?

Answer: The British Council is owned by the British government. For this reason, the pressure to be profitable is low, compared to that on a private company like Virgin Atlantic. Also, Virgin Atlantic planes take off whether they are full or not. Every empty seat is lost revenue, and so Virgin Atlantic is under greater time pressure.

- How can you reduce the leverage of Virgin Atlantic?

Answer: Ensure that the information session is two months before the school year in the United Kingdom. This way, attendees will be under more pressure to choose an airline, and Virgin Atlantic will see a greater return, should it invest in sponsorship.

- How can Virgin Atlantic reduce the leverage of the British Council?

Answer: Form a coalition with other airlines. If possible have another airline offer a false bid to sponsor the event, and then—a few weeks or even days before the event—pull out. Virgin Atlantic can then offer to assist at a much lower price—perhaps at 2006 prices.

■ What additional benefits could you include that have little value to the British Council but greater value to Virgin Atlantic?

Answer: Allow Virgin Atlantic to speak at the event, in order to highlight the benefits of choosing their airline (safety and convenience). Also, the British Council could offer the e-mail list of all attendees and the right to use its logo on future follow-up e-mails.

■ Who are the stakeholders in this negotiation?

Answer: The parents are the obvious stakeholders. Price of tickets will be important, but more important than that will be safety. This is where Virgin Atlantic can highlight its safety record over the domestic airlines. Other stakeholders include British banks, hotels, car rental companies, and universities, who could ultimately become future sponsors of this information session.

Bibliography

Bailenson, J. N., and Yee, N. (2005). "Digital Chameleons: Automatic Assimilation of Nonverbal Gestures in the Immersive Virtual Environments." White paper, Psychological Science, Department of Communication, Stanford University.

Cialdini, R. B. (1984). *Influence: The Psychology of Persuasion* (New York: HarperCollins).

Collins, J. C., and Porras, J. I. (1994). *Built to Last* (New York: HarperCollins).

Fang, Y., and Hall, C. (2003). "Chinese Managers and Motivation for Change: The Challenges and a Framework." Proceedings of the 15th Annual Conference of the Association for Chinese Economics Studies Australia (ACESA). Macquarie Graduate School of Management, NSW, Australia.

Fisher, R., and Ury, W. (1983). *Getting to Yes* (New York: Penguin Books).

Gitomer, J. (2003). *The Sales Bible* (Hoboken, N.J.: Wiley).

Hewitt-Gleeson, M. (1990). *Newsell* (North Brighton, Vic., Australia: Wrightbooks).

Hewitt-Gleeson, M. (2006). *WOMBAT Selling* (Prahran, Vic., Australia: Hardie Grant Books).

Hoefstede, G. (1980). *Culture's Consequences: International Differences in Work-Related Values* (Beverly Hills, Calif.: Sage).

Hoefstede, G. (1991). *Cultures and Organizations: Software of the Mind* (Berkshire, England: McGraw-Hill).

Hoefstede, G. (2009). "Cultural Dimensions; China," n.d. Accessed February 20, 2010, at www.geert-hofstede.com/hofstede_china.shtml.

Lum, G. (2004). *The Negotiation Fieldbook* (New York: McGraw-Hill).

Miller, R. B., Heiman, S. E., and Tuleja, T. (1998). *The New Strategic Selling* (New York: Business Plus).

Ministry of Education, Department of Planning. (2003). *Report of Education Statistics* 1, no. 26 (China).

Pace, R. W., and Faules, D. F. (1994). *Organizational Communication* (Needham Heights, Mass.: Allyn & Bacon).

Index